AMERICAN ART
FROM THE COLLECTION OF THE
WORCESTER ART MUSEUM

With an Introduction by Richard Stuart Teitz

April 27 — June 24, 1979

AMON CARTER MUSEUM
FORT WORTH

The Amon Carter Museum was established in 1961 under the will of the late Amon G. Carter for the study and documentation of westering North America. The program of the museum, expressed in publications, exhibitions, permanent collections, and special events, reflects many aspects of American culture, both historic and contemporary.

Library of Congress Catalog Card Number: 79-84788
International Standard Book Number: 0-88360-031-5

Cover: *Mrs. Elizabeth Freake and Baby Mary,* c. 1674

Introduction

The Worcester Art Museum was founded in February, 1896, because of the impetus of the community's leading business figure, Stephen Salisbury III. He invited a group of ten women and thirty-six men to join him in forming a corporation dedicated to art and art education to be known as the Worcester Art Museum. At that initial meeting Salisbury made known his intent to give the Corporation $100,000 and a tract of land. A year later a contract for $90,000 was let to erect a granite and brick building 128 x 56 feet, three stories high, and on May 10, 1898 the Museum was formally opened with a special loan exhibition.

On November 16, 1905 Stephen Salisbury died at the age of seventy. At a special meeting the same day, an appreciation was voted by the Museum's Board of Directors: "Mr. Salisbury exemplified to an unusual degree some of the noblest qualities of one of the best types of the New England gentleman and scholar. . . . Lover of antiquity, of hospitality, of good learning, of good men, he was always ready to support with patient and pious zeal every worthy cause. . . . Having means, taste and opportunities which would have inclined many men to selfish leisure, he really lived a life of laborious and almost austere service for the good of others in public and private. . . . He was not only the founder of the Museum — he was also, so to speak, its cherishing father, and the cordial, interested friend of all its officers. Recognizing, as early as 1891, Worcester's need of such an institution, he first proposed a gift of a comparatively small lot of land and ten thousand dollars, and then, as with characteristic openness and teachableness of mind . . . he enlarged these gifts to our present ample lot of more than two acres, and one hundred thousand dollars for a building. With his peculiar self-negation, refusing to have the institution bear his name, or to have any share in its control, he magnanimously put it into the hands of others, for the benefit of all the people of Worcester. Gift after gift has since followed from his liberal hand until now, the Museum has a site, a building, an endowment, a collection, a spirit that gives it a recognized standing among similar institutions in the land."

Salisbury left almost his entire estate of nearly four million dollars to the Worcester Art Museum, and after a lengthy suit pressed by his relatives, the Massachusetts Supreme Court ruled the bequest go to the Museum. That gift provided the endowment income to operate the Museum, acquire outstanding works of art in several fields, and create a reserve for future physical expansion. In addition, Stephen Salisbury had both given in his lifetime and bequeathed several portraits of his family by such distinguished American artists as Gilbert Stuart, Chester Harding, and Danish-born Christian Gullager. These works of art constituted the genesis of a collection of eighteenth-century New England portraits, now one of the most highly prized features of the Worcester Art Museum.

Major additions to the American collection came in the 1910s and 1920s. Included in this group are Washington Allston's 1813 painting *Christ Healing the Sick*; Joseph Badger's full-length representation of John Larrabee; a distinguished portrait of Theodore Atkinson by the Anglo-American painter Joseph Blackburn; John Singleton Copley's 1763 likeness of Sarah Tyler Savage; *Charles Cotesworth Pinckney* by James Earl; and a pair of portraits of the children William and Mary Ann Carpenter by James Earl's more famous brother Ralph. Also acquired in these years were Charles Willson Peale's 1792 portrait of Charles Pettit; Edward Savage's portrait of his young son; *Margaret Siddons* by Thomas Sully; and Whistler's study of his mistress Maud Franklin, entitled *The Fur Jacket*.

Opportunities to add important American paintings diminished, and the collection has seen few additions in the past two decades, although among these is the acknowledged masterpiece of the collection, the 1674 portrait of Mrs. Elizabeth Freake and her six-month-old daughter Mary, painted in Boston by the unknown but highly gifted "Freake Limner." With the meteoric rise in prices for American paintings of the eighteenth and nineteenth centuries, it appears unlikely the Worcester holdings can be extensively augmented. Therefore, the institution considers itself particularly fortunate in having early established this rich collection.

It is a further pleasure to be able to share Worcester's American treasures with the Amon Carter Museum of Western Art and to make them accessible to the people of Texas. We, in our turn, are delighted to be able to present the major holdings of the Amon Carter Museum, the works of Frederic Remington and Charles M. Russell and their colleagues which reflect the expansion and development of the American West. It is our hope that the residents of both Massachusetts and Texas are enriched by this exciting exchange program.

Richard Stuart Teitz
Director, Worcester Art Museum

Unknown artist (active in Boston in the 1670s)

Mrs. Elizabeth Freake and Baby Mary
Oil on canvas, c. 1674 (42-1/2 X 36-3/4 in.) Gift of Mr. and Mrs. Albert W. Rice, 1963.134

Beginning with the increasing power of the landed and mercantile wealth, there was a rapid development of all colonial arts. For those who wanted to make visible their rising station in life, portraiture was particularly popular. Like furniture, silver, pewter, and glass, portraiture was serviceable; effigies were equal to other household items. Well-to-do merchants, sea captains, and officials with their wives and children, as well as clergymen, made up the long list of colonial portraits. If one were to judge society by these portraits alone, one would imagine genteel prosperous folks not in the least hampered by strenuous difficulties of settling in the colonies.

Two of the most familiar paintings in the Museum's collection, the two Freake portraits are acknowledged to be the outstanding examples of early colonial portraiture. If, as family tradition maintains, the infant shown here is Mary, eighth child of John and Elizabeth Freake, who was born in May of 1674, then the painting must have been executed in November of that year, since the inscription gives her age as six months. Both these portraits remained in the possession of their descendants until they entered the collection in 1963.

The artist of both works is unknown. It is thought he must have been a painter who came from England or the continent soon after the Massachusetts colony was founded, to practice the craft of sign and house painting. He turned to portraiture only much later, when the growing prosperity of the colony created a demand. His style is related to the sixteenth-century style of Elizabethan portraiture.

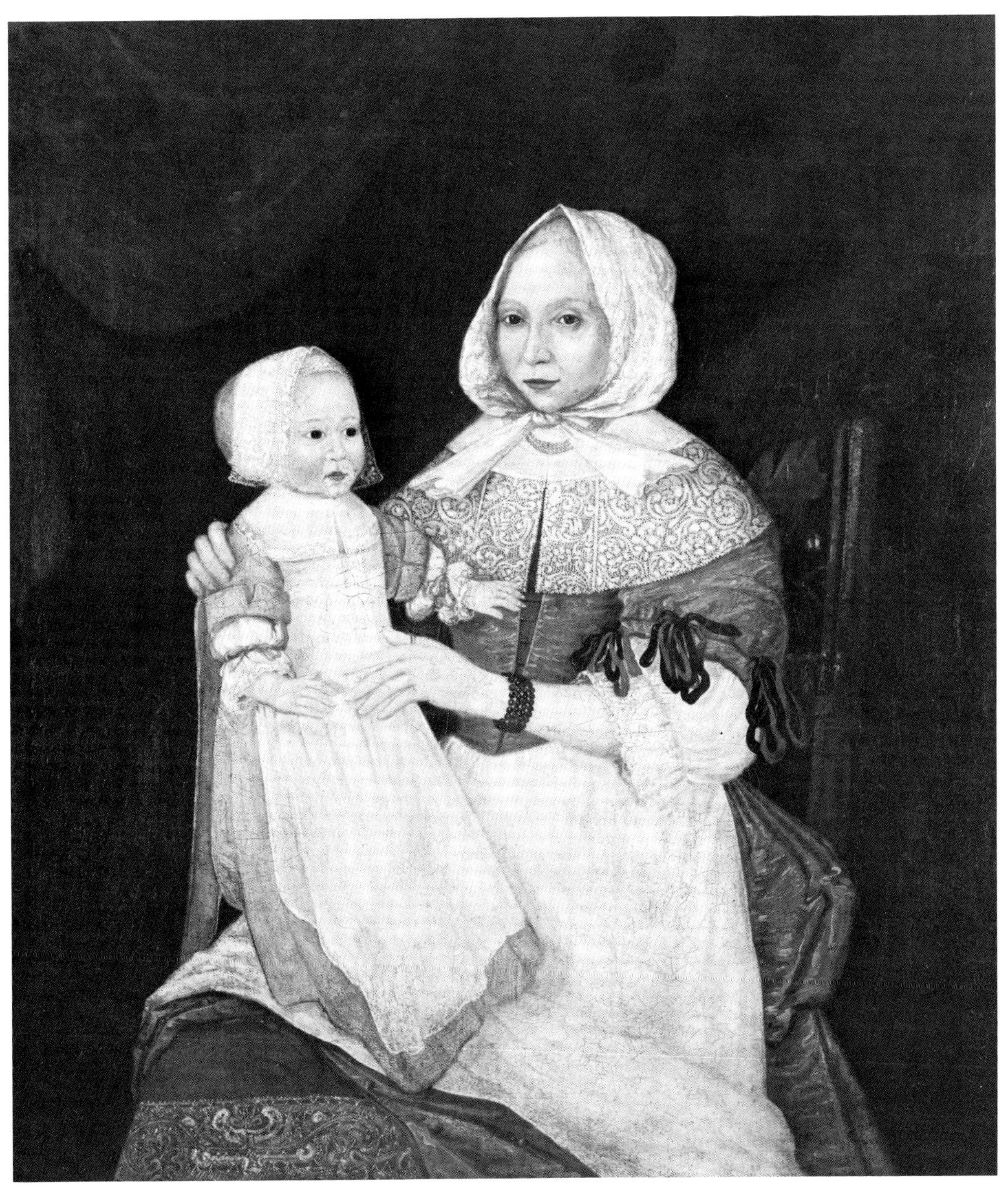

Unknown artist (active in Boston in the 1670s)

John Freake

Oil on canvas, c. 1674 (42-1/2 x 36-3/4 in.) Museum purchase, Sarah C. Garver Fund, 1963.135

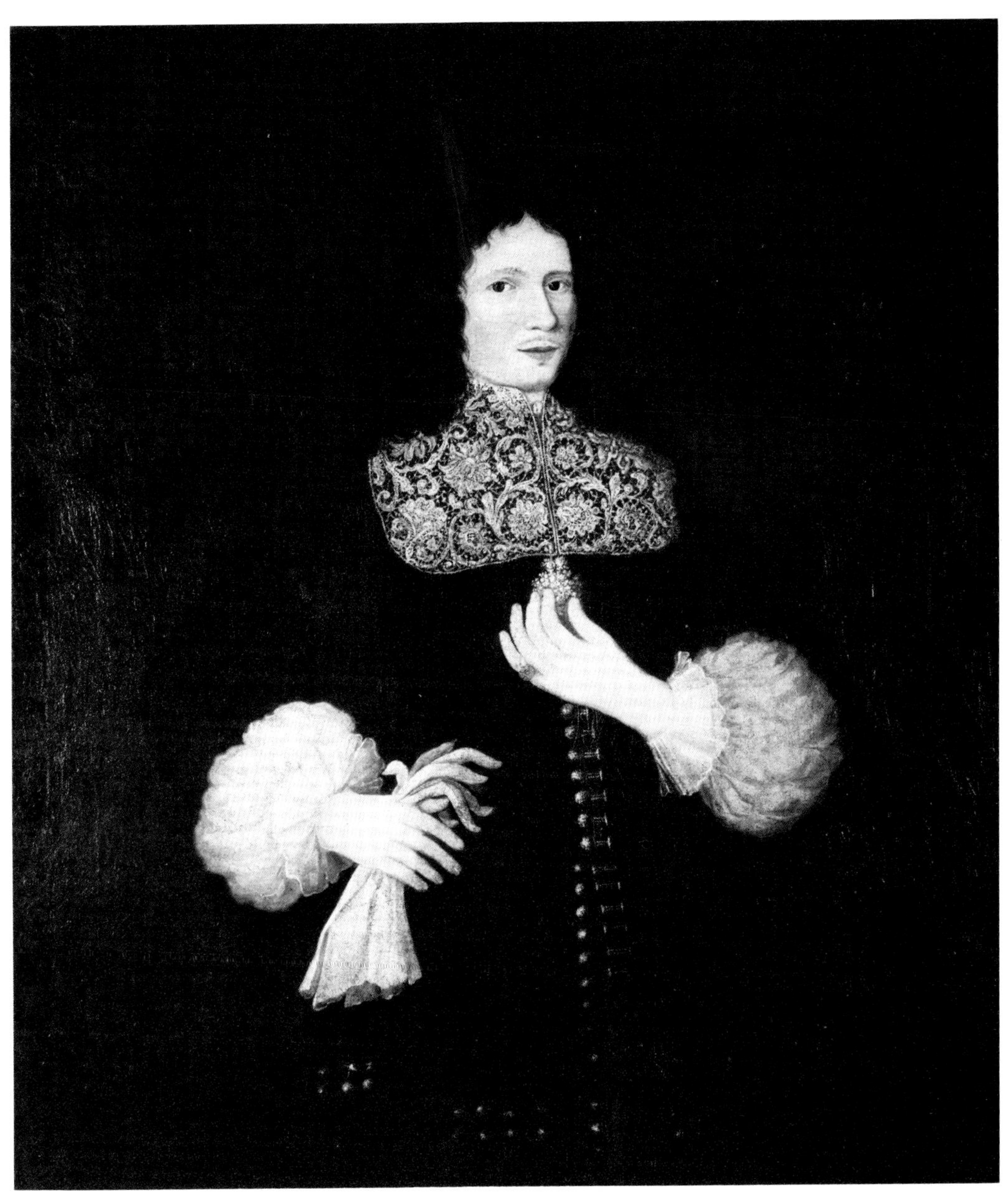

Thomas Smith, American (active c. 1680)

Self-Portrait
Oil on canvas (24-1/2 x 23-3/4 in.) Museum purchase, 1948.19

Almost at the same time as the portraits of the Freake limner, there were several distinctly different likenesses painted to which the name of Thomas Smith has been attached. In his self-portrait and in that of his daughter, Maria Catherine, Thomas Smith offers a more general approach to costumes allowing greater concentration upon facial expressions. While the Freake portraits reflect a linear, two-dimensional quality with finely detailed and decorated costumes, the two Smith portraits reveal less about surface qualities of costumes but tell more about form and mass. This more advanced approach in the Smith portraits represents a definite break with the medieval tradition of decorative effect in favor of the Renaissance attempts to represent figures in space by use of light and shade. Smith's colors have no bright jewel-like qualities; they are somber and quiet, varying in intensity and value to suggest the three-dimensional quality of forms.

In addition to all the traditional "stage properties" in the self-portrait, the tassled, drawn curtain, the skull and the manuscript, we are offered a glimpse of a naval engagement in the upper left corner. The ships are flying Dutch and English flags while one of the flags of the forts in the foreground has three crescents on a red ground, suggesting a Moorish fortification on the African coast. We must assume that this vignette was intended to indicate Thomas Smith's background as a captain. And, as a scholar in his study, he follows a seventeenth-century convention of poetry and meditation.

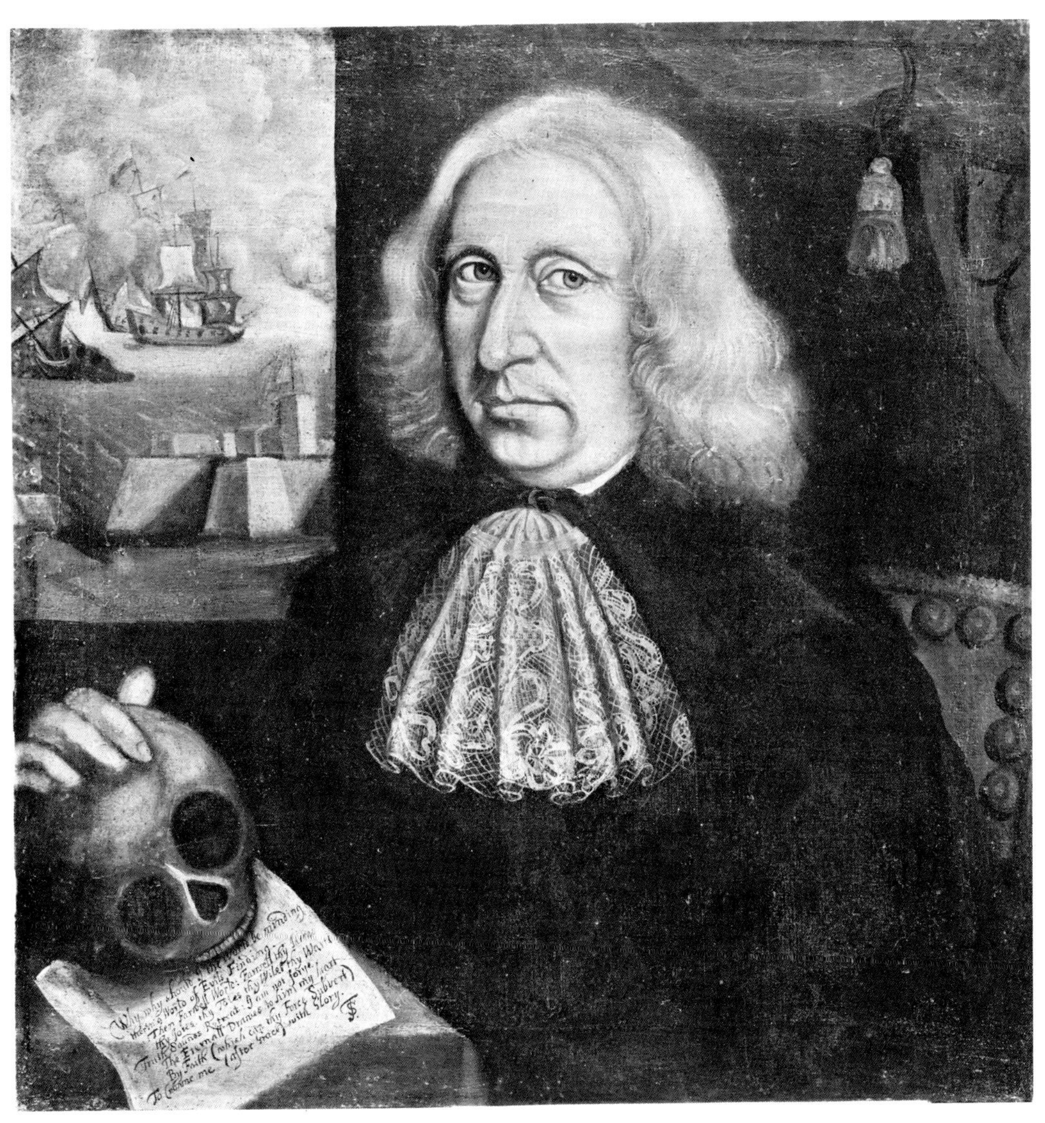

Why why should I of Death be minding
Meere a World of Evills Finding (by Land)
Then Farwell World Farwell my Land
My Joves thy Toes thy Wiles thy Ware
Truth Sounds Retreat: I am not forye
The Eternall Drames to him my heart
By Faith (which cutt my Force Subvert)
To Crowne me (after grace) with Glory.
S.

John Smibert, British (1688-1751; lived in America after 1729)

Mrs. Henry Ferne (Elizabeth Dayrel)
Oil on canvas, 1724 (50-3/8 x 40-1/4 in.) Museum purchase, 1958.40

Shortly after John Smibert arrived in the colonies in 1729, he became the most influential immigrant artist of the American colonial period. Trained at the Academy in London, Smibert had the opportunity to visit Florence and Rome. In Boston, Smibert introduced himself to his new clientele by exhibiting all the works he had brought with him from England; his originals as well as those he had copied in Italy. Included were his copies of Raphael's *Madonna dell'Impannata,* Poussin's *Continence of Scipio,* and van Dyck's *Portrait of Cardinal Bentivoglio* and some of his plaster casts of antique sculptures such as the *Venus de Medici* and possibly *Laocoön*. This was in fact New England's first art exhibition.

The artist's likeness of the widow Elizabeth Ferne, portrayed in her formal mourning attire, was painted at the sitter's home in Lincolnshire, England in 1724. It had remained on the wall of Mrs. Ferne's ancestral manor in the company of many other family portraits until it was purchased by the Worcester Art Museum in 1958.

The very same pose of the sitter appears in at least two other known compositions by different artists which confirms a British practice, prevalent later in America, of borrowing and copying compositions from published portrait prints. Eighteenth-century artists felt free to incorporate already-well-established compositions, poses, costumes and backgrounds, into their own works. Another reason for this practice was that English as well as American patrons usually sat for their faces only and left the artist to fill in the rest of the compositions.

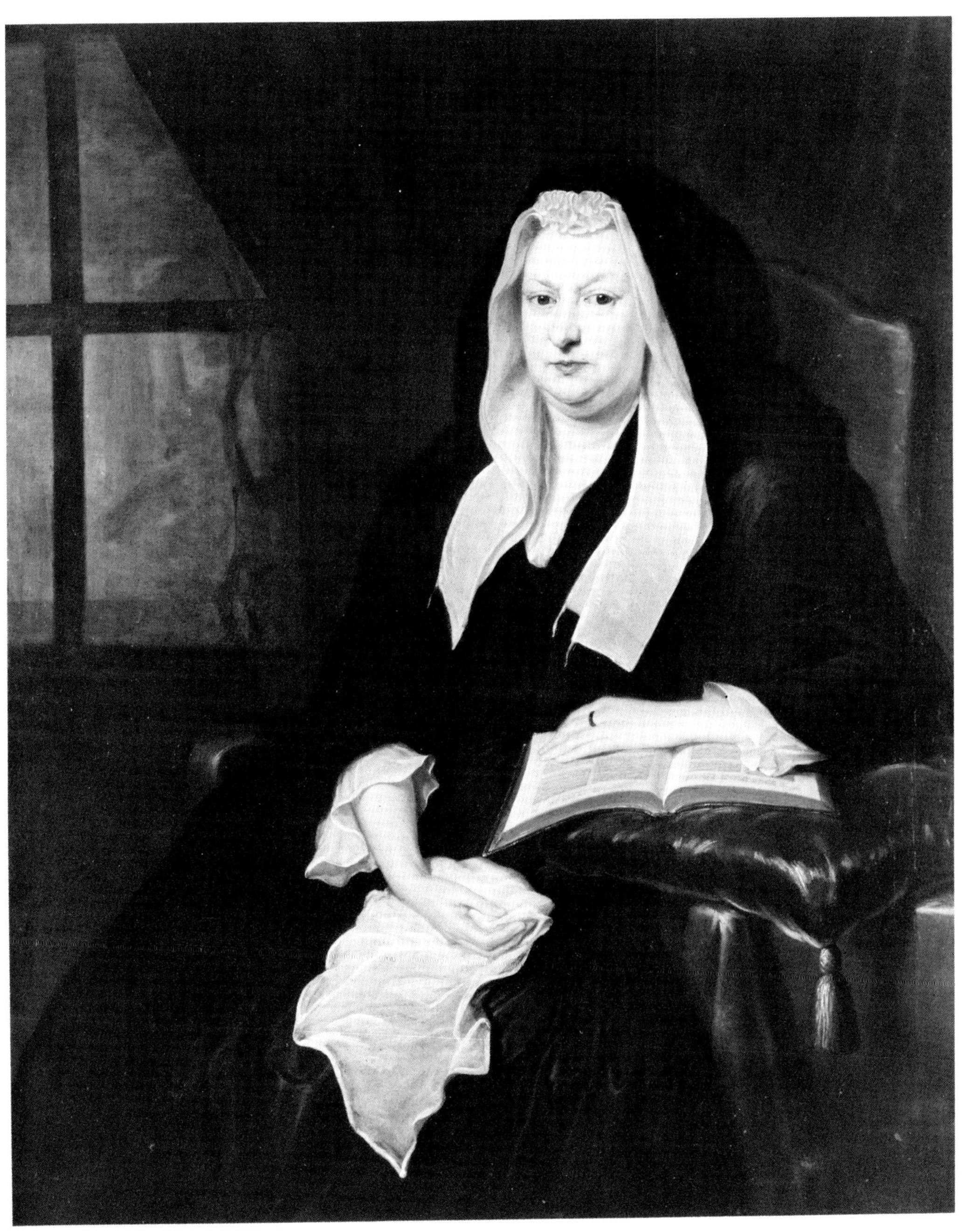

Joseph Badger, American (1708-1765)

Rebecca Orne
Oil on canvas (25-7/8 x 20-3/4 in.) Eliza S. Paine Fund in memory of William R. and
Frances T. C. Paine, 1971.101

Lois Orne
Oil on canvas (25-5/8 x 20-3/4 in) Eliza S. Paine Fund in memory of William R. and
Frances T. C. Paine, 1971.102

Of the first documented native-born artists, Joseph Badger contrasts
with the foreign-trained John Smibert in almost every aspect imagi-
nable. Born in Charlestown, he came from humble origin and was
trained to be a glazier. As an artist he was entirely self-taught with little
or no chance to study other paintings. Unable to gain social rank, he
remained in straitened circumstances throughout his life. Apparently,
he left Boston only once to paint a house in nearby Dedham. Between
the years 1748 and 1758, this provincial colonist was Boston's leading
artist. After his death, Badger was completely forgotten for over a
century. The first two American histories of American art in 1834 and
1867 have no mention of him.

Badger, like many colonial painters, felt he could portray children
most flatteringly if he painted them as respectable little adults. This
rarely yields a relaxed or natural pose. Dressed in their best Sunday
clothes, as are all of Badger's portrait subjects, these two earnest young
ladies hold their favored treasures, a pet squirrel and a wooden rattle.

Lois's later marriage to Dr. William Paine brought her his wedding gift
of forty-five pieces of Paul Revere II silverware, thirty of which survive
in the Worcester Art Museum. These, together with pastel likenesses of
Paine and his sister Hannah Babcock, remain in Paine's home city,
Worcester, though he was denounced as a Loyalist, driven to England
and only returned with Lois in 1793 to his house "The Oaks," still
standing today.

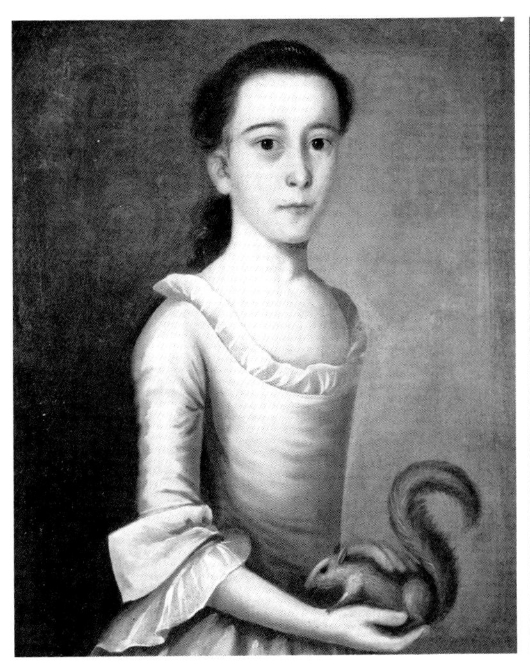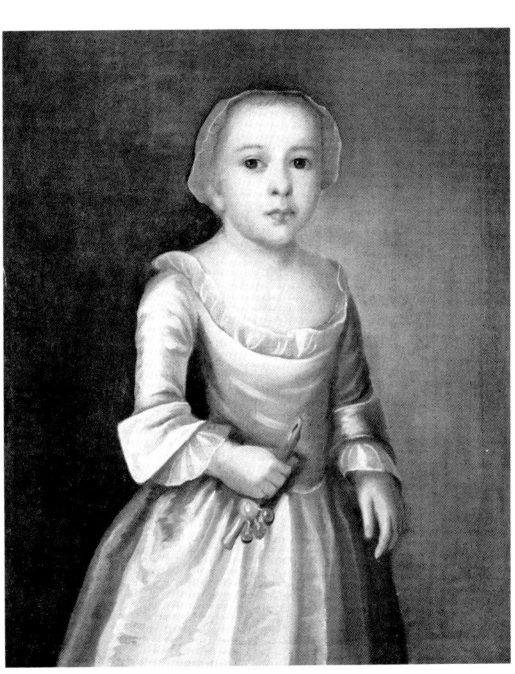

Joseph Badger, American (1708-1765)

Captain-Lieutenant John Larrabee
Oil on canvas (83-5/8 x 51-1/8 in.) Museum purchase, 1920.53

Of all Badger's work that has come to light, this portrait is the largest and in many ways most significant. Of the three standard portrait poses, seated, three-quarter length, and full-length, the latter was undertaken least often. One of the reasons for avoiding the imposing full stance was its association with English royalty. Influenced, as were all colonial artists, by English prints, and especially those of Kneller, Badger developed rather specific and easily recognizable manners for his portraits. One hand typically rests on the hip with two fingers outstretched, holding back an overcoat; the other hand, if not hidden, holds or indicates some object associated with the subject's profession.

Captain John Larrabee (1686?-1762) was noted for his long public service as Captain-Lieutenant of Castle-William of Boston Harbor. The notice of his death in the *Boston News-Letter* of February 11, 1762, tells us much about the kind of man the Bostonians held in such high esteem:

> Thursday last departed this life after a few Days illness, universally lamented, that very worthy servant of the Province Captain-Lieutenant John Larrabee, of Castle-William aged 76 years. His uprightness and Integrity, his generosity and publick spirit, his plain heartedness and Humanity, as well as freedom from Guile, recommended him to all. His Name was dear to the Soldiery of the Castle who loved and revered him as their friend and father, and so sensible was the Province of his Worth and Merit, that he was continued as Captain-Lieutenant and Victualler of Castle-William for more than 40 Years to his Death. And his whole Character may be summed up in that comprehensive sentence — a sincere Christian.

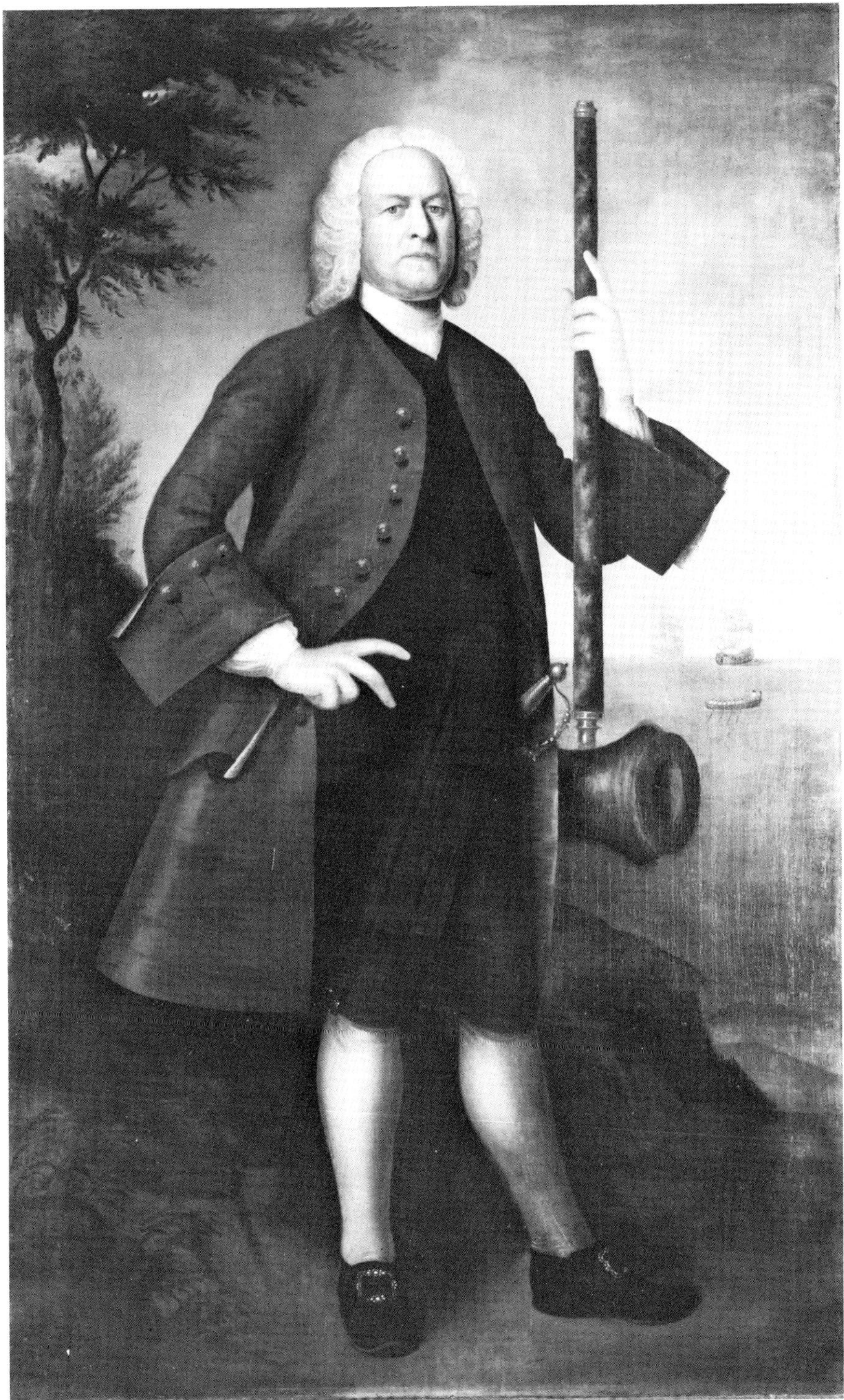

Jeremiah Theus, American, b. Switzerland (1716-1774; lived in America after c. 1735)

Portrait of a Man, Possibly the Honorable Isaac Holmes
Oil on canvas, 1775 (29-7/8 x 25 in.) Museum purchase, 1938.78

Jeremiah Theus was born in Switzerland and came to Charleston, South Carolina, in 1735. He advertised himself as a painter five years later, but where or from whom he received his training is not known.

In 1755 Theus produced two nearly identical portraits, this one and another now in The Charleston Museum. The sitter may be the Honorable Isaac Holmes, a member of His Majesty's Council in Charleston. He died in 1751, so if it is he who is represented the portraits must be taken from an earlier likeness and not from life. The portraits descended in two branches of his family, which supports the identification.

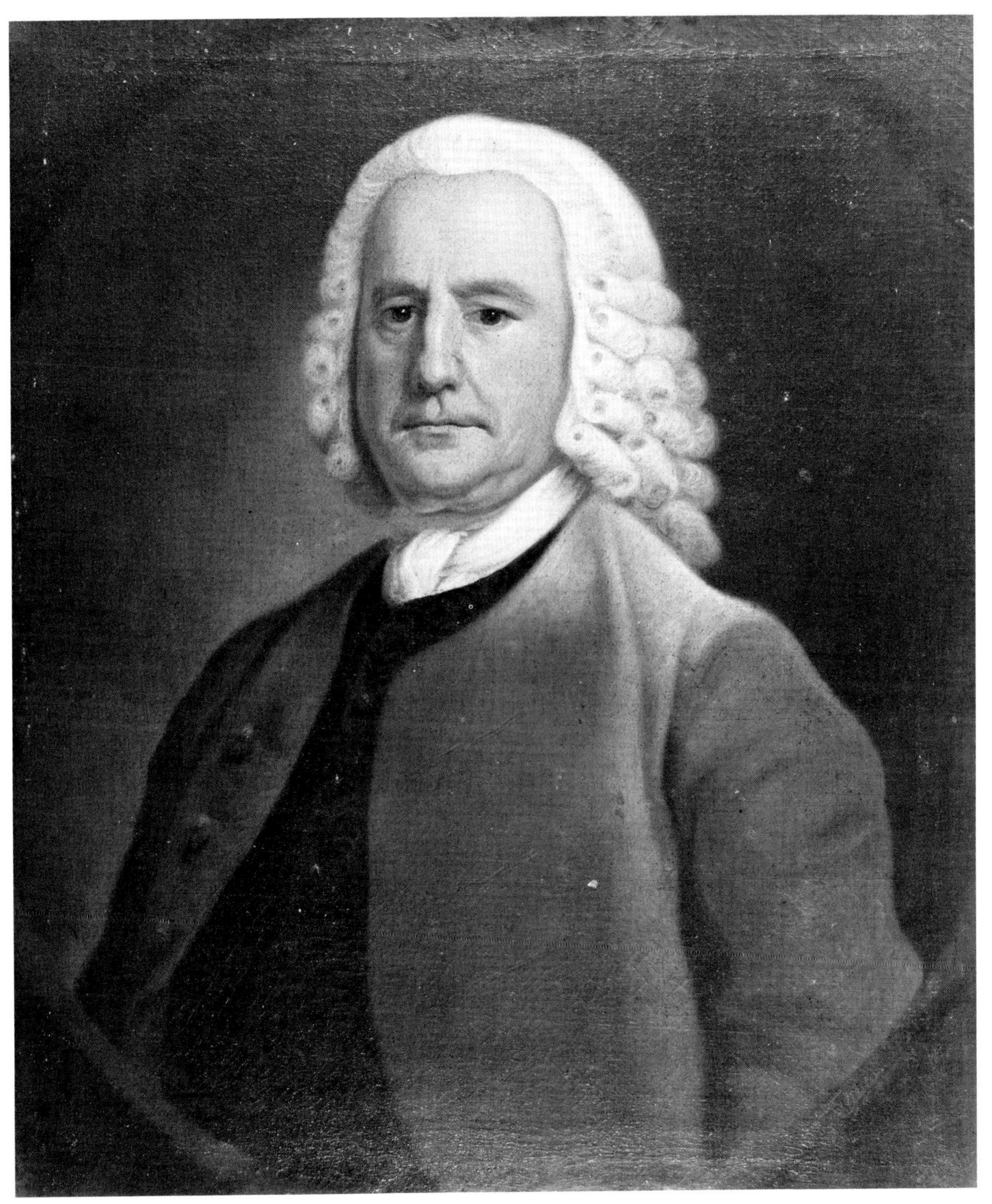

Joseph Blackburn, British (active in America c. 1754-1763)

Colonel Theodore Atkinson
Oil on canvas (50 x 40-1/4 in.) Museum purchase, 1918.13

Like the itinerant artists John Wollaston and Jeremiah Theus, Joseph Blackburn accepted commissions from various corners of the colonies. Apparently on a painting tour from England, Blackburn painted portraits in Newport, Boston, and Portsmouth. Within the span of a decade here, he painted more than eighty likenesses of well-to-do colonists. By 1764 he had returned to England, where he remained active until his death.

His portrait of Theodore Atkinson (1697-1779) is one of his more successful male portraits. Usually Blackburn preferred to show his considerable ability depicting the jewelry, feathers, lace, silks, velvets, and gold- and silver-trimmed costumes worn by ladies. Certainly worthy of his attention was the well-known, sometimes controversial New Hampshire Colonel Atkinson. Contemporary records refer to him as "one of the ablest men of his time . . . largely interested in starting new towns, furnishing the money for the settlers and taking his pay in land." In spite of his great wealth and his affiliation with the British Crown, he was so universally admired and respected that no attempt was made to confiscate his property during the time of the Revolution. In his will he gave two hundred pounds to the St. John's Episcopal Church in Portsmouth, the interest to be forever expended for bread to this day.

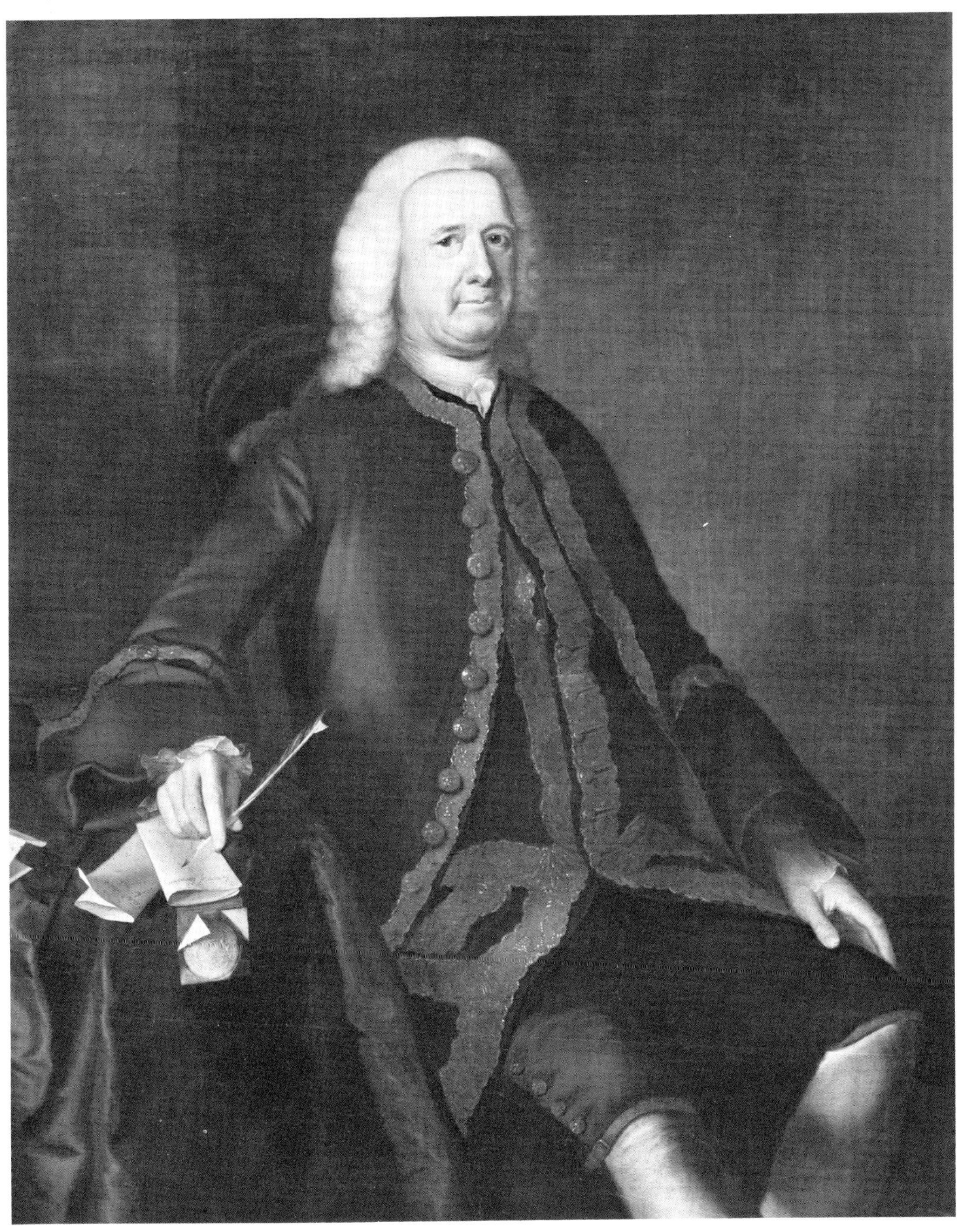

Joseph Blackburn, British (active in America c. 1754-1763)

Mrs. John Bours (Hannah Babcock)
Oil on canvas, 1759 (50-1/8 x 40-1/8 in.) Bequest of George Nixon Black, 1929.23

Hannah Babcock was sixteen when Joseph Blackburn painted this portrait of her in 1759. She was the daughter of Dr. and Mrs. Joshua Babcock of Westerley, Rhode Island. Three years later she was to marry John Bours of Newport, whose portrait by Copley is owned by the Worcester Art Museum.

This picture shows Blackburn's reliance on English models for his portraits. The background, costume, and pose of the sitter are all copied from an engraving after a painting by Thomas Hudson, a British portraitist.

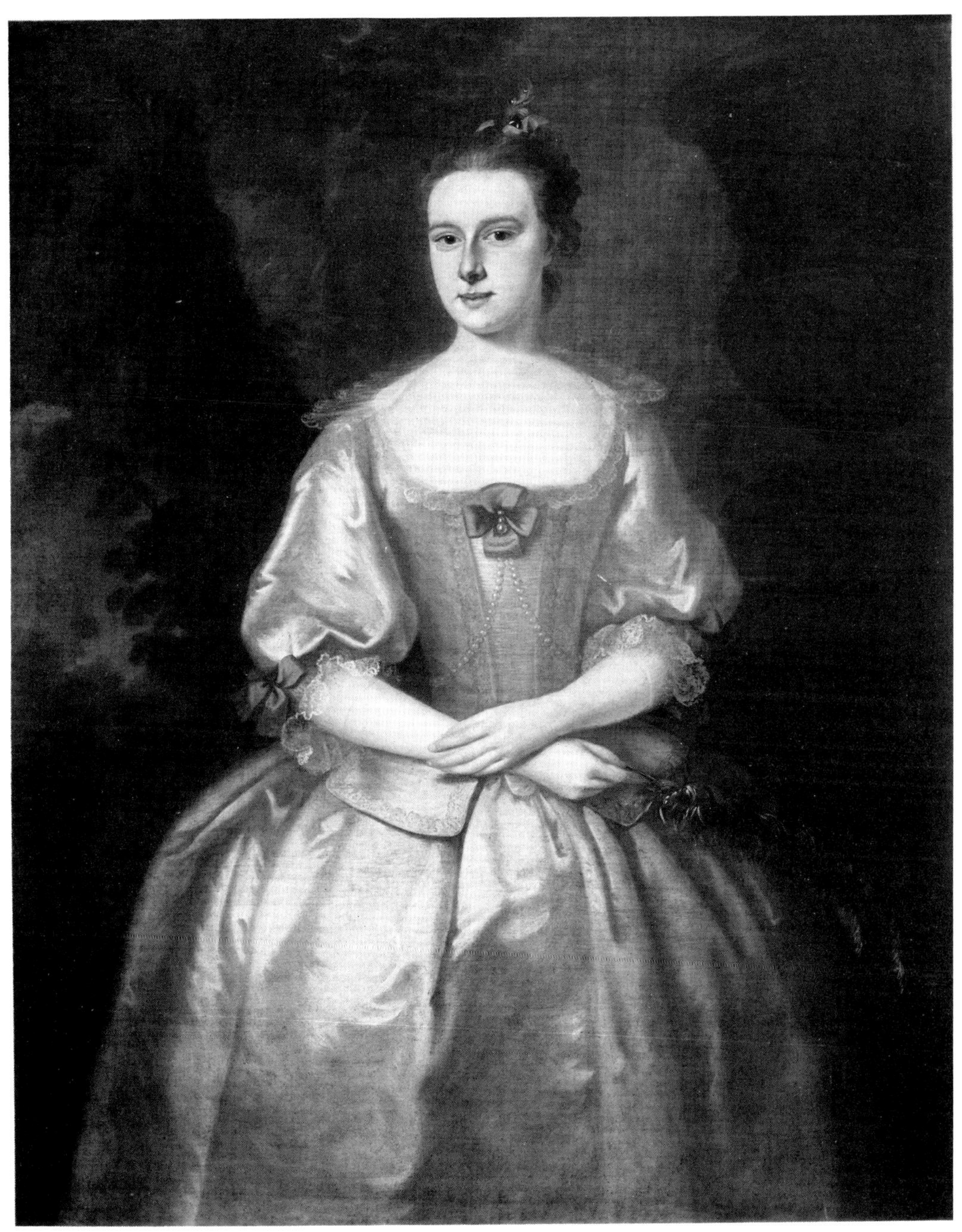

John Wollaston, British (active in America 1749-1758 and 1767)

Ann Gibbes (Mrs. Edward Thomas)
Oil on canvas, 1767 (30-1/8 x 25-1/8 in.) Museum purchase, 1946.1

The aristocracy of English Loyalists in the South insisted that the best painting could be done only in London or elsewhere in the Old World. As a result, the development of local painters in the South lagged far behind New England where the "codfish aristocracy" was quite content to have its likenesses taken by limners near at hand. Of those few artists who managed to solicit commissions in the South, Wollaston and Theus are represented here.

Like Theus, Wollaston sought his commissions from plantation owners in the South. After his activities there between 1749 and 1758, his travels took him to India where he remained for six years. Before his final return to England, he visited the colonies once again in 1767, the year he painted this portrait of Ann Gibbes, a debutante of the southern aristocracy. The fact that he portrayed over three hundred of the most prominent colonists in the South (more than Feke, Smibert and Blackburn together) attests to his popularity and influence.

In London Wollaston was known as a "drapery painter" who, in the tradition of the Van Dyck-Kneller workshop painted costumes and draperies in the background to complete the portraits started by the so-called "face painters." Together with Blackburn, Wollaston brought the contemporary English Rococo portrait style of Hudson and Highmore to the colonies. Many of their pleasing and delicate portraits, varying little in their poses, served as attractive decorations for the colonial Georgian mansions.

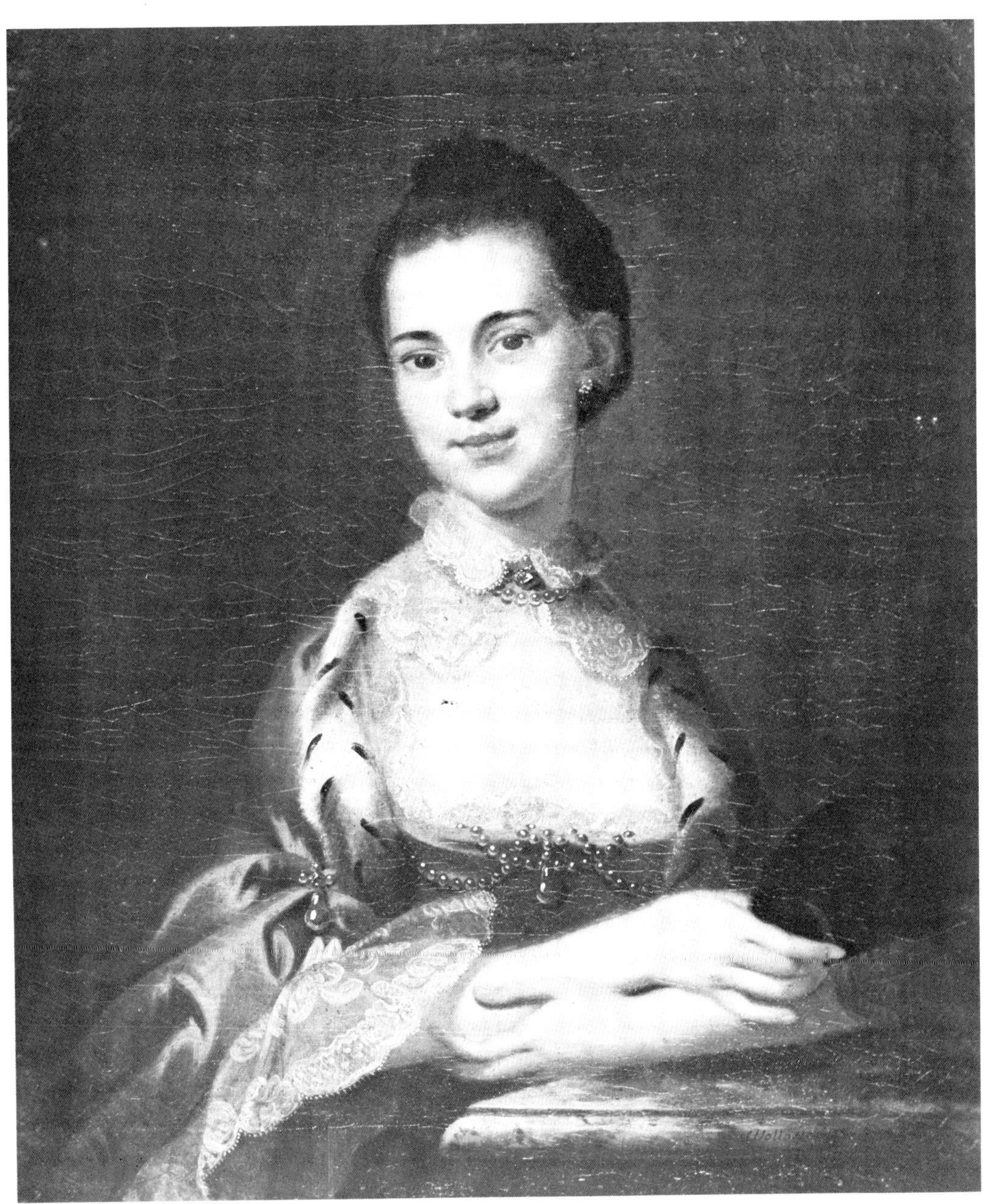

John Singleton Copley, American (1737/8-1815; lived in England after 1775)

John Bours
Oil on canvas, c. 1761 (50-1/4 x 40-1/8 in.) Museum purchase, 1908.7

As a young boy John Singleton Copley received instruction in the art of mezzotint printmaking from his stepfather Peter Pelham. While he and Joseph Blackburn worked in Boston at the same time, it cannot be proven that Copley was trained by Blackburn or by John Smibert, although these two artists certainly influenced his painting. Starting his career at the age of fifteen, Copley quickly excelled in both technical competence and in his thorough understanding of his sitters' psychological make-up.

Despite overwhelming early success, Copley was dissatisfied. In a letter to his friend Benjamin West in London, he laments: "Was it not for preserving the resemblance of particular persons painting would not be known in this place. . . . The people generally regard it no more than any other useful trade . . . like that of a Carpenter tailor or shew maker, not as one of the most noble Arts in the world." By the time the patriot Paul Revere was distracted by war, Copley had left for England, never to return to America.

John Bours (1734-1815), whose wife Hannah Babcock was painted by Blackburn, was one of Newport's most civic-minded citizens and President of the Redwood Library there. During the trying Revolutionary period after the evacuation of the British troops from the island, Bours acted as the lay reader at Trinity Church, keeping the church doors open for the remaining members of the congregation.

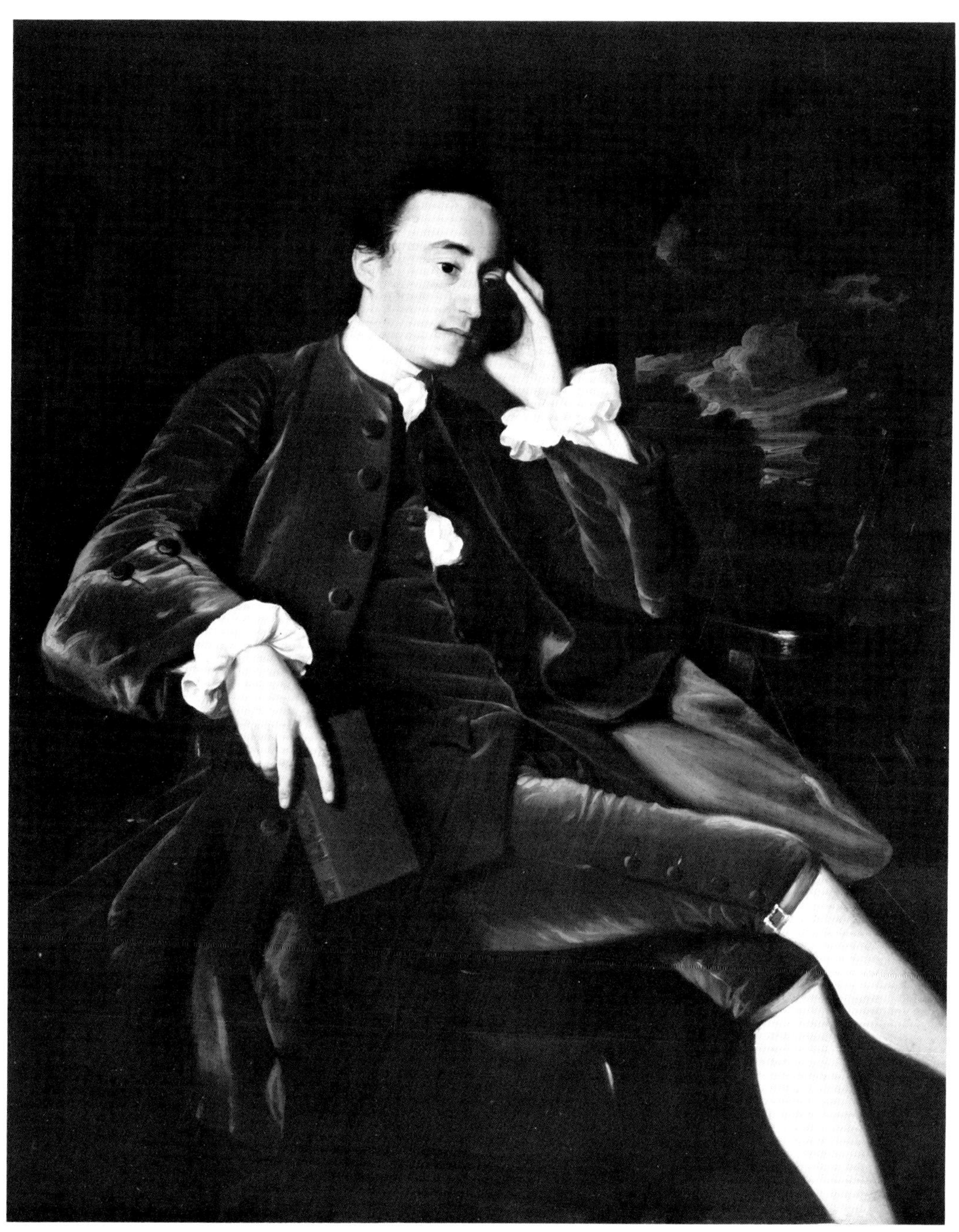

John Singleton Copley, American (1737/8-1815; lived in England after 1775)

Mrs. Samuel Phillips Savage (Sarah Tyler)
Oil on canvas, 1763 (50-1/8 x 40-1/2 in.) Museum purchase, 1916.51

This likeness of Mrs. Samuel Phillips Savage (1717/8-1764) was acquired directly from Savage descendants in 1916. The Savages were merchants of provisions, selling mainly tea, sugar, molasses, swordfish, raisins, and flour. Probably afflicted by taxes, it is said that Mr. Savage took part in the historic "Liberty Tree" protest and the decision to launch the Boston Tea Party.

Copley did not hesitate to borrow suitable compositions from English mezzotint prints. As the rather stiff and formal posture of Mrs. Savage, as well as the foreign-looking countryside in the background suggest, some undiscovered print might have given Copley the inspiration for this particular setting. Perhaps Copley, first trained by his stepfather, the engraver Peter Pelham, was particularly ready to accept the English print as a guideline and source of information. The painter's preference for mezzotints rather than line engravings was twofold: mezzotints were larger in size and thus easier to copy, and they gave the image in tone rather than line.

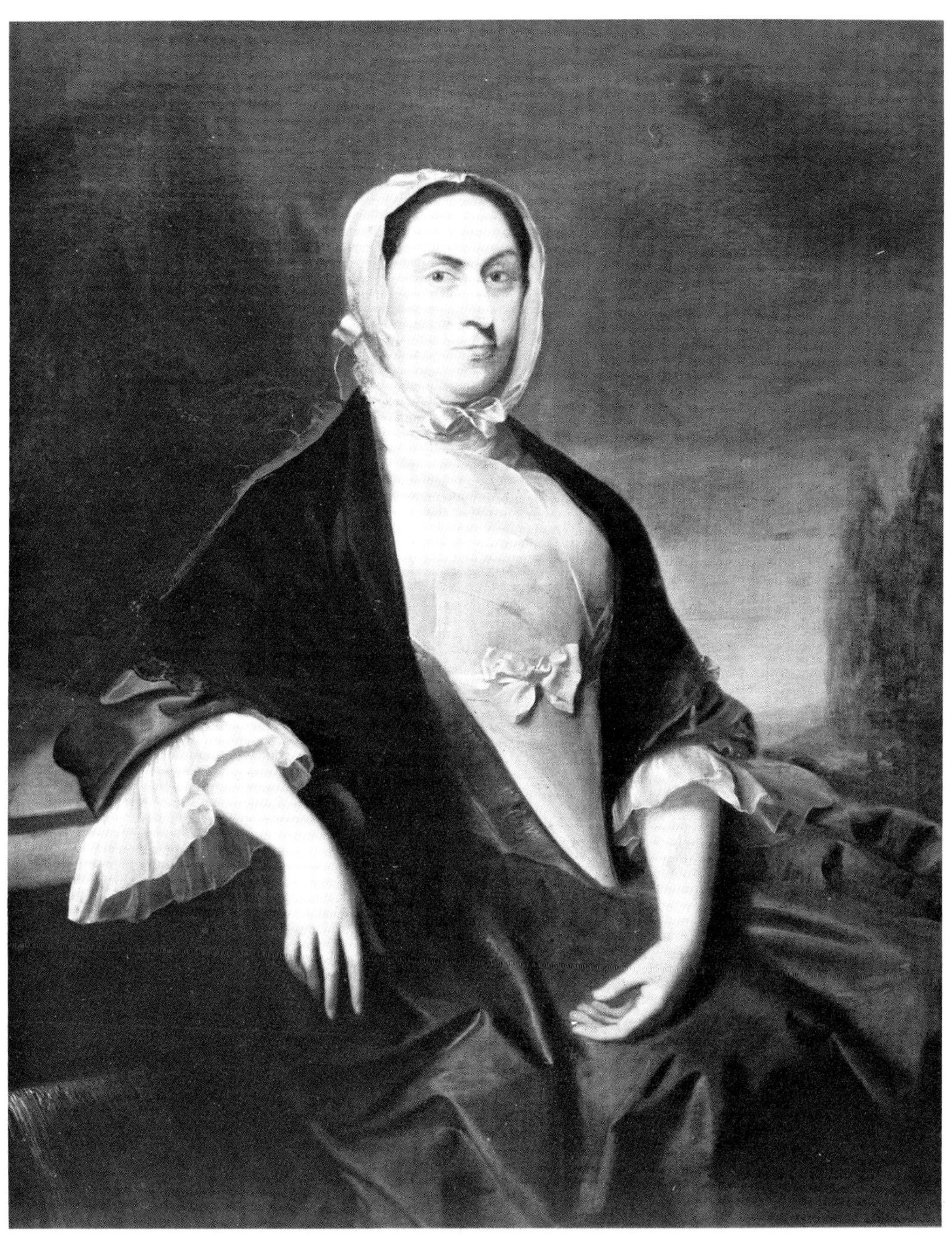

John Singleton Copley, American (1737/8-1815; lived in England after 1775)

Mrs. John Murray (Lucretia Chandler)
Oil on canvas, 1763 (49-7/8 x 40 in.) Bequest of H. Daland Chandler, 1969.37

In the same year he painted Mrs. Savage, Copley painted the beautiful Mrs. John Murray (1730-1768), who grew up in Worcester as one of seven sisters known locally as the Seven Stars. Lucretia married the Honorable John Murray of Rutland as his third wife in 1761. Here Copley's direct dependence upon an English mezzotint print has been identified. Not only the composition, but also the subject's elegant, lace-trimmed gown and her poised pose have been derived from John Faber's mezzotint of 1746 after Hudson's portrait of the Right Honorable Mary, Viscountess Andover. The formal English garden in the background, equally unsuitable for a New Englander, attests further to Copley's source. But how, we must ask, did Copley manage to render this figure and the textural qualities of silk, velvets, and laces so convincingly while the background still lacks any depth and definition? How could he possibly paint his impressions of the effects of light and shade so successfully without having these materials actually in front of him?

The striking inconsistency between the figures and the background can best be explained by Copley's supposed device of requesting his models to do the copying. Rather than trying to copy a gown from a black-and-white print, Copley may have asked his sitters to have their dressmakers duplicate a gown from a mezzotint. Dressmakers were already in the habit of copying English costumes from imported fashion prints. The sitter could then easily enough provide the proper gesture or pose. It was, of course, another matter to paint an impression of a landscape, a challenge not taken up until more than a century later.

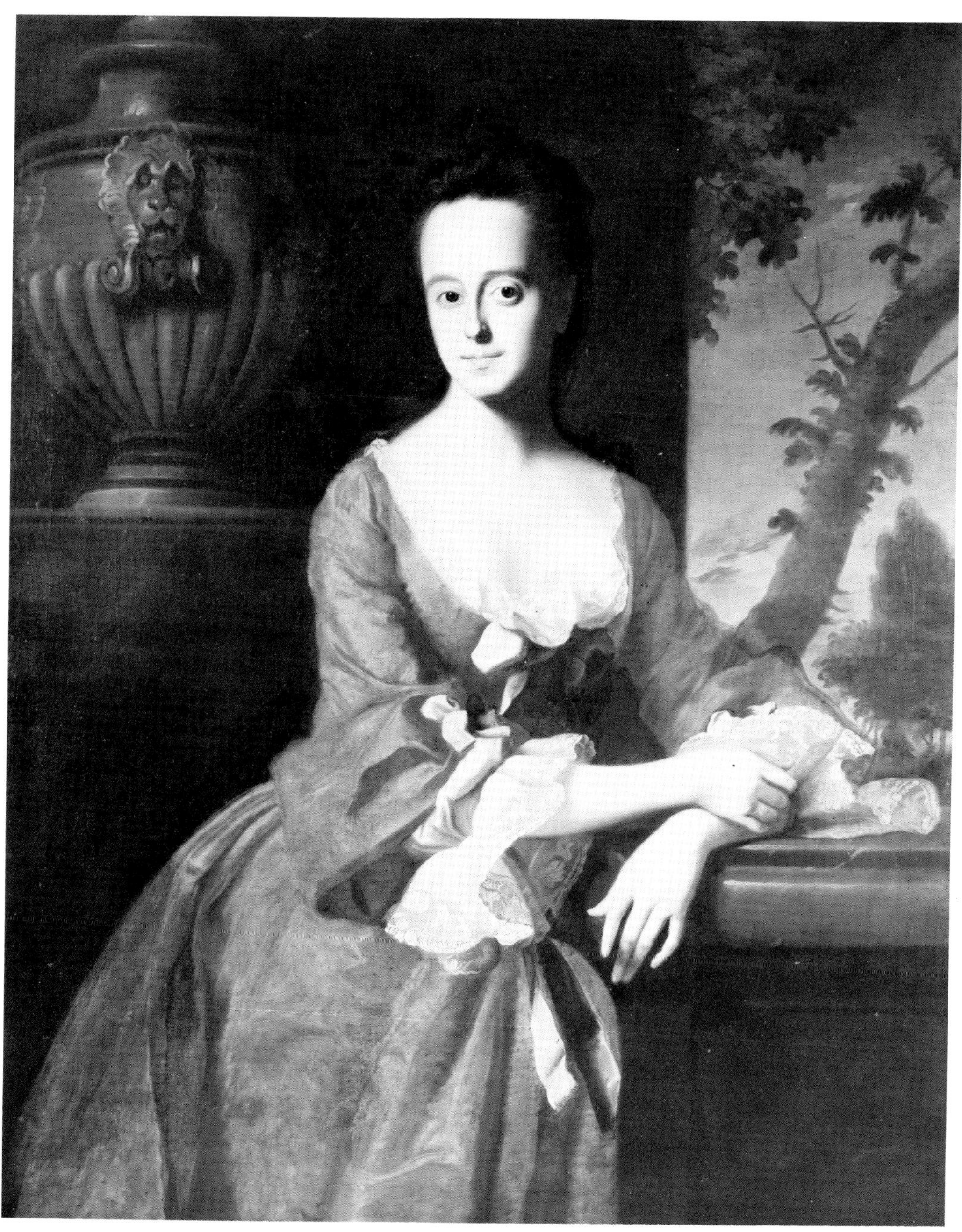

Benjamin West, American (1738-1820; lived in England after 1763)

Pharaoh and His Host Lost in the Red Sea
Oil on canvas, (38-1/4 x 30 in.) Museum purchase, 1960.18

West rose from humble beginnings as a limner in Lancaster, Pennsylvania, to become a founder of the British Royal Academy and an official painter to George III. He lived in London and gained a tremendous reputation for his grand history paintings. He had a large school, and many Americans trained under him.

This boldly conceived sketch was a preliminary study for a painting which was to have formed part of a large cycle for George III's private chapel in Windsor Castle. The finished painting is now lost, and the chapel was never completed. The turmoil and painterly exuberance of this sketch are characteristic of West's late style but are quite removed from his earlier, classicizing manner.

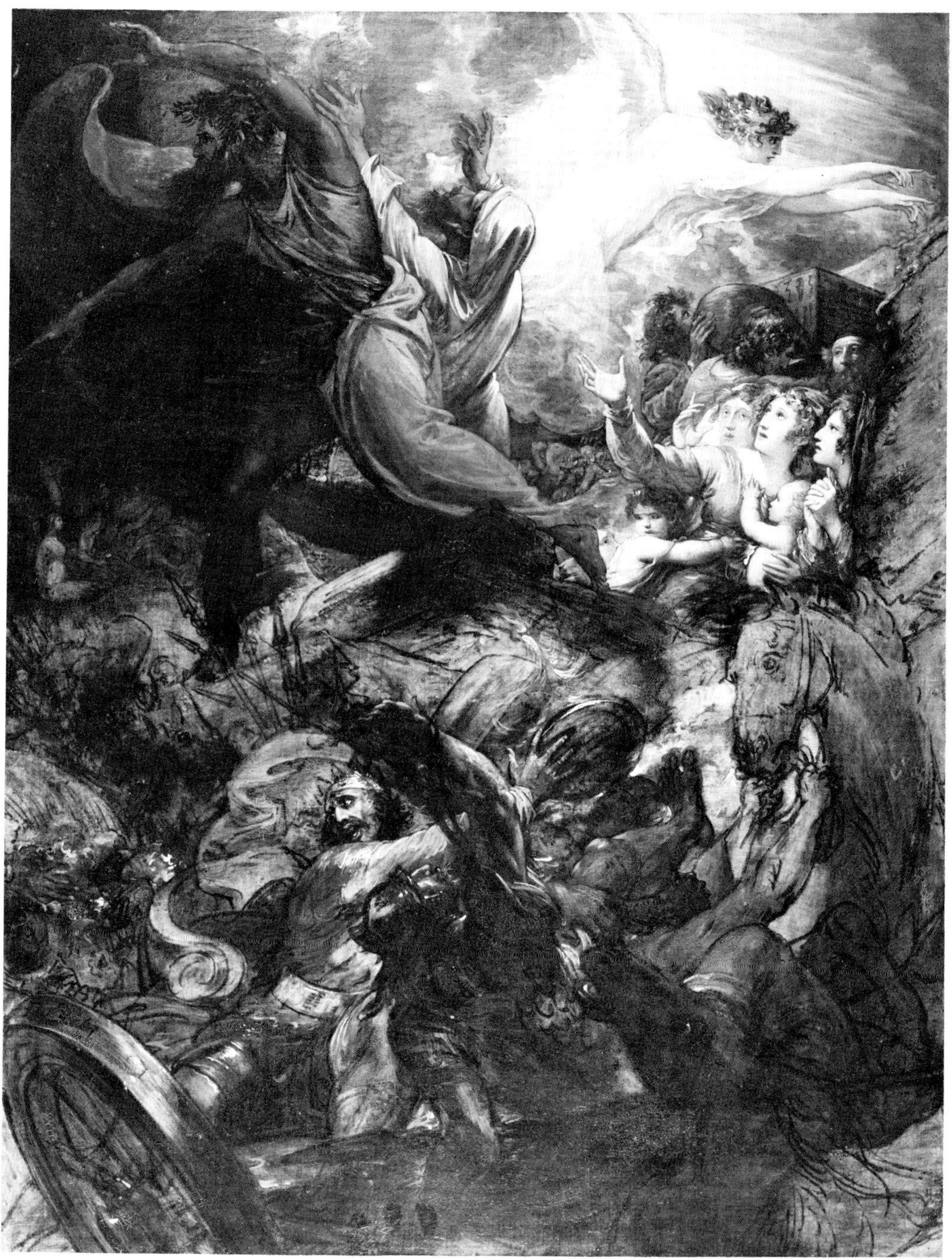

Unknown artist (18th century)

Overmantel from the Reverend Joseph Wheeler House, Worcester
Oil on panel (24-7/8 x 60 in.) Gift of Charles A. Aiken in memory of Mrs. Henrietta L. P.
Aiken, 1954.15

This homestead, long since disappeared, is that of the Reverend
Joseph Wheeler House (center) formerly on Main Street, Worcester,
almost opposite the present First Unitarian Church. So many such
panel paintings have fallen into oblivion that it is helpful to see the
donor's historical notes of the Wheeler panel discovery:

> ... the panel painting had never been seen by my mother, but she
> had been told as a child by her mother that there was a picture
> under the white paint, and, as children we often amused ourselves
> by tracing the dim outlines of trees and houses, appearing as slight
> irregularities on the white surface. No one dreamed at that time that
> the covering surface could be removed, but, before the house was
> demolished my mother learned that it was possible, and when the
> panel was removed gave it into the hands of John D. Smith, an
> antiquarian and old furniture restorer, who removed the paint to
> the best of his ability. ..."

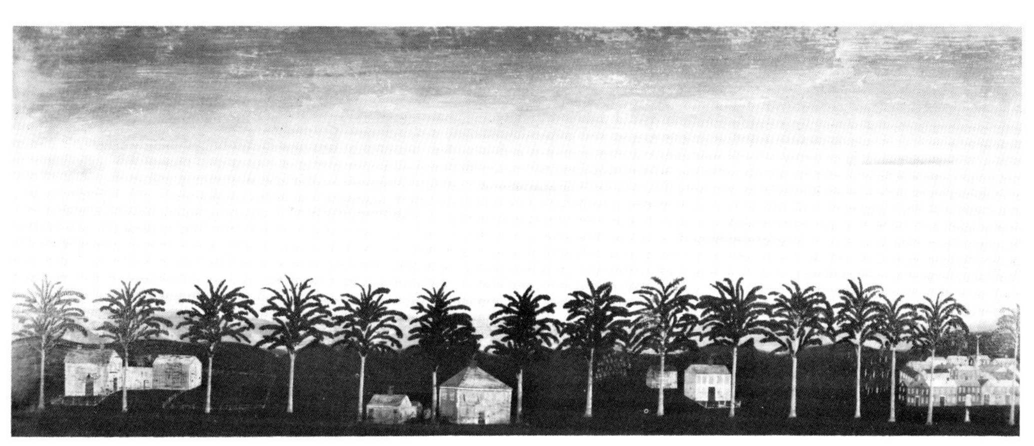

Ralph Earl, American (1751-1801; lived in England 1778-1785)

William Carpenter
Oil on canvas, 1779 (47-7/8 x 35-5/8 in.) Museum purchase, 1916.1

Ralph Earl was born in Shrewsbury, Massachusetts, and was raised in a part of Leicester which later became Paxton. In 1774 he opened a studio at New Haven, Connecticut. Earl declined to serve in the rebellion and was banished from Connecticut. He succeeded in leaving America in 1778 in the company of Captain John Money, Quartermaster General to Burgoyne, who had been permitted to return to England under the surrender terms at Saratoga in 1777. On his arrival in London, Earl made the acquaintance of Benjamin West. Earl then settled in Norfolk near Captain Money's home where the Museum's portraits of *William Carpenter* and *Mary Ann Carpenter* were painted in 1779. During the ensuing years, Earl sought to make a place for himself in the English portrait school, but after the close of the American Revolution, he realized that his native land offered him greater opportunity to practice his art. He returned to America in 1785 to take up portraiture in New York and in New England. During the remaining years of his life, Ralph Earl painted many of the nation's Revolutionary figures.

William Carpenter (1767-1823) was twelve when he sat for this portrait, a full-length, seated study. The boy has a quiet and thoughtful presence; he pauses from reading a book. The paint has been smoothly applied to the broad areas of the picture while the details have been deftly handled, as in the almost transparent lace and the brass buttons of sunburst design.

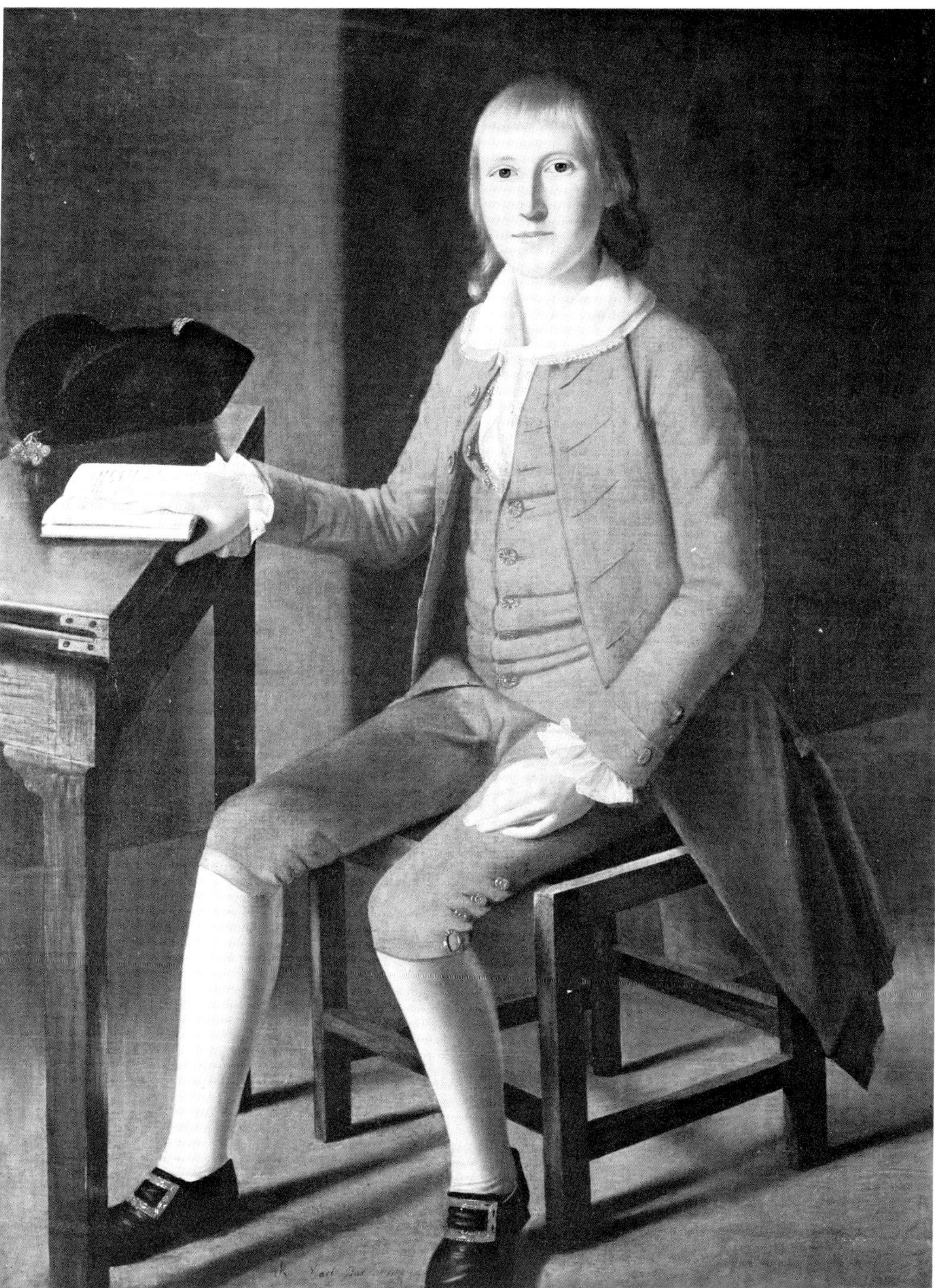

Ralph Earl, American (1751-1801; lived in England 1778-1785)

Mary Ann Carpenter
Oil on canvas, 1779 (47-1/4 x 35 in.) Museum purchase, 1916.2

Mary Ann Carpenter was fourteen when Earl painted her portrait. Little is known about her, except from what has been revealed through the parish register at Aldeby, which records her baptism on January 12, 1766, and her marriage on September 24, 1784, to Thompson Forster, a London surgeon.

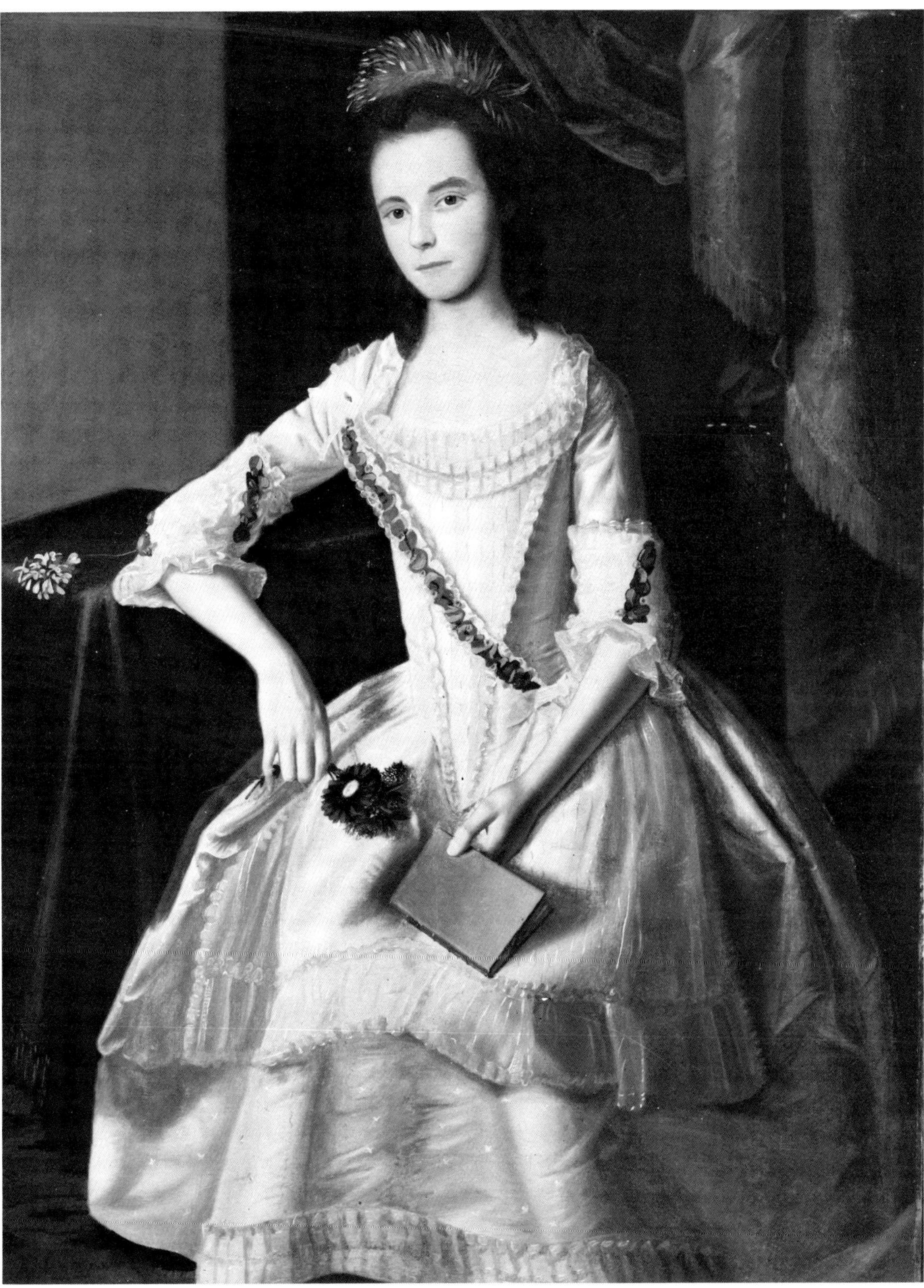

Ralph Earl, American (1751-1801; lived in England 1778-1785)

Looking East from Denny Hill
Oil on canvas, 1790s (45-3/4 x 79-3/8 in.) Museum purchase, 1916.97

Looking East from Denny Hill is one of the first pure landscapes to be produced in the early republic (prior to this, landscape had taken the form of overmantels). Ralph Earl was commissioned by Colonel Thomas Denny to undertake the painting when the colonel planned to move from his family homestead on Denny Hill in Leicester, Massachusetts, to a newly built home in the same town. Thomas Denny wanted to take with him a picture of the view he had enjoyed from childhood. The landscape was painted at the close of the eighteenth century within a few years of Earl's death in 1801. The artist has created the vision of a summer landscape where farmers work late into the day to take in their hay. Muted and modulated earth colors dominate the scene in which white buildings serve to accent the receding terrain. The land had long been cleared and settled when Earl made the painting in the 1790s. Boundaries were defined by tree lines, stone walls, and rail fences. The post road to Boston appears in the middle-ground leading to Worcester with its spires of the First Parish or Old South Church and the Second Parish Church. Shrewsbury lies beyond Worcester on the horizon.

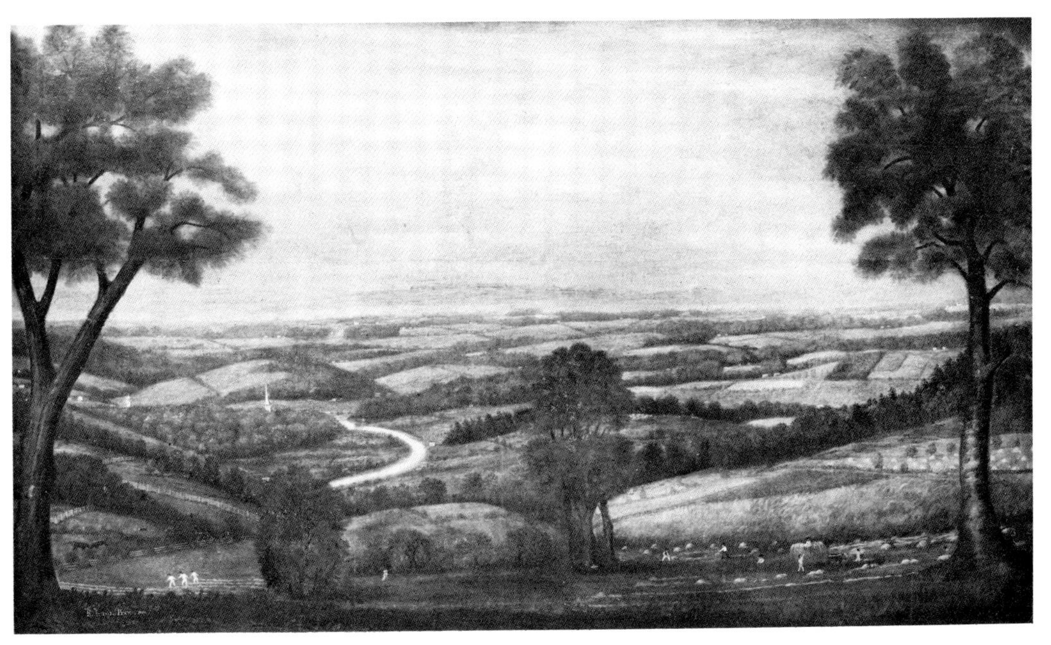

Edward Savage, American (1761-1817)

The Savage Family
Oil on canvas, c. 1779 (25-3/4 x 34-1/2 in.) Gift of William A. Savage, 1964.7

The Savage Family was painted before Edward Savage turned twenty. The artist stands at the left in a dressing gown with palette in hand. Seated next to him is his grandfather Edward Savage, who emigrated from northern Ireland early in the eighteenth century to settle in Rutland, Massachusetts. The painter's parents, Seth Savage (1732-1807) and Lydia (Craige) Savage (d. 1816), are next. The nine children in the artist's generation are present in the picture, but a tenth child has curiously been included. The names of the Savage children are known; however, their birth dates are unknown. Thus, their identification has yet to be made. The painting descended from the artist's younger brother Joseph to the donor, William A. Savage.

Primitive elements are evident in the work. This may be seen in the disproportionate rendering of the heads and the bodies. The fact that the floor tiles recede in size from left to right in a steep plane implies that Savage may not have known the rules of perspective.

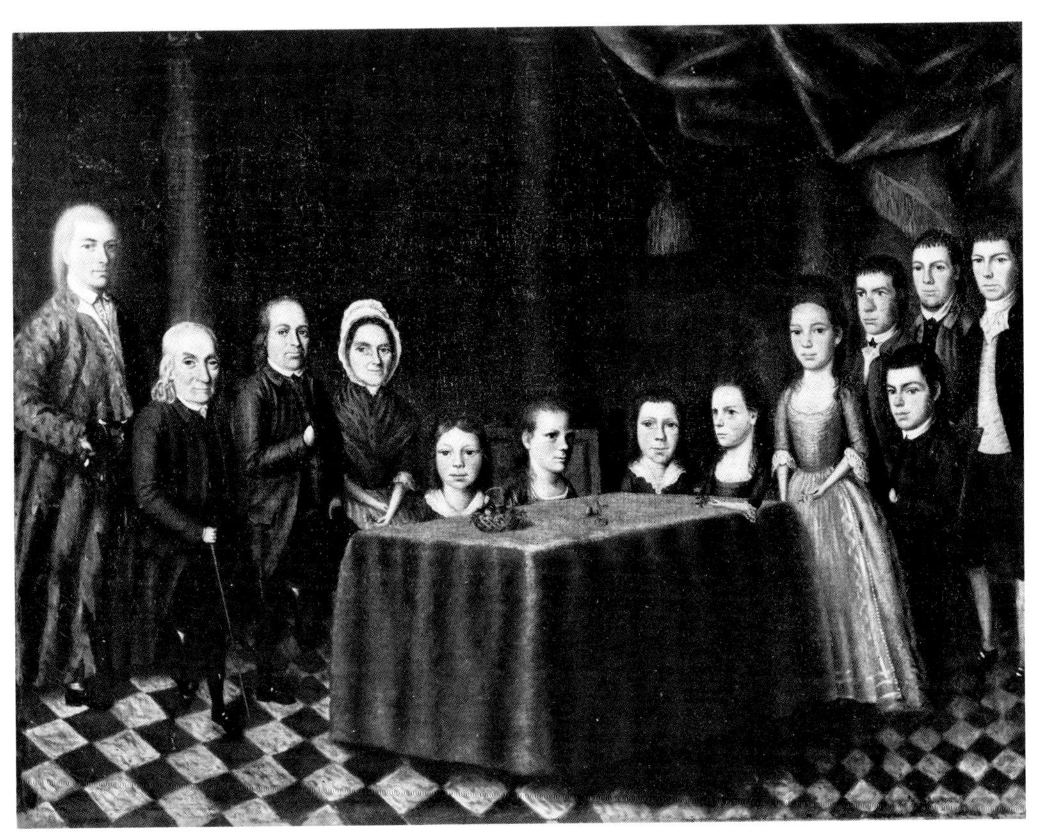

Edward Savage, American (1761-1817)

Edward Savage, Jr.
Oil on canvas (30-1/4 x 25 in.) Museum purchase, 1924.38

This portrait of his son was probably painted more than twenty years after Savage's early portrait of his family. The difference between the two pictures dramatically illustrates Savage's development from a young amateur painter, struggling to capture likenesses but unsure of proportions or lifelike drawing, to a sure professional, skilled in composition and the manipulation of light and color, sensitive to the mood and appearance of his subject.

Edward Savage, Jr., was born in Boston on August 25, 1795. He married in 1831, and died in Springfield, Massachusetts, in 1858.

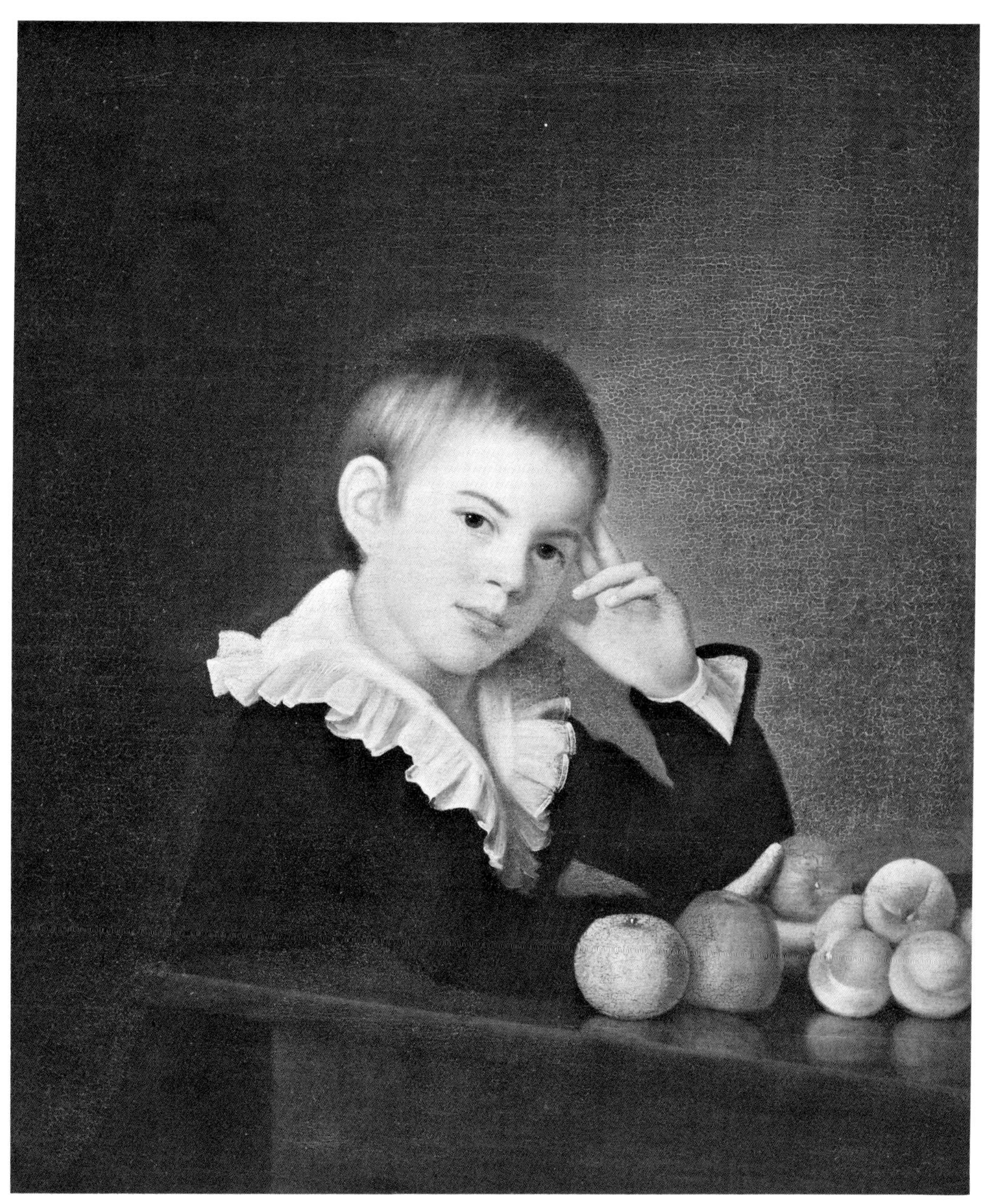

Christian Gullager, American, b. Denmark (1759-1826; lived in America after 1786)

Mrs. Nicholas Salisbury (Martha Saunders)
Oil on canvas, 1789 (36 x 28-3/4 in.) Gift of Stephen Salisbury III, 1901.22

Gullager was born in Denmark in 1759, studied at the Royal Academy in Copenhagen, and came to America in 1786. He worked in Boston, New York, and Philadelphia, where he died in 1826.

Mrs. Salisbury (1704-1792), here aged 84, was the mother of Mrs. Norton Quincy, Mrs. Daniel Waldo, Samuel Salisbury, and Stephen Salisbury I. She was the great-grandmother of Stephen Salisbury III, principal founder of the Worcester Art Museum.

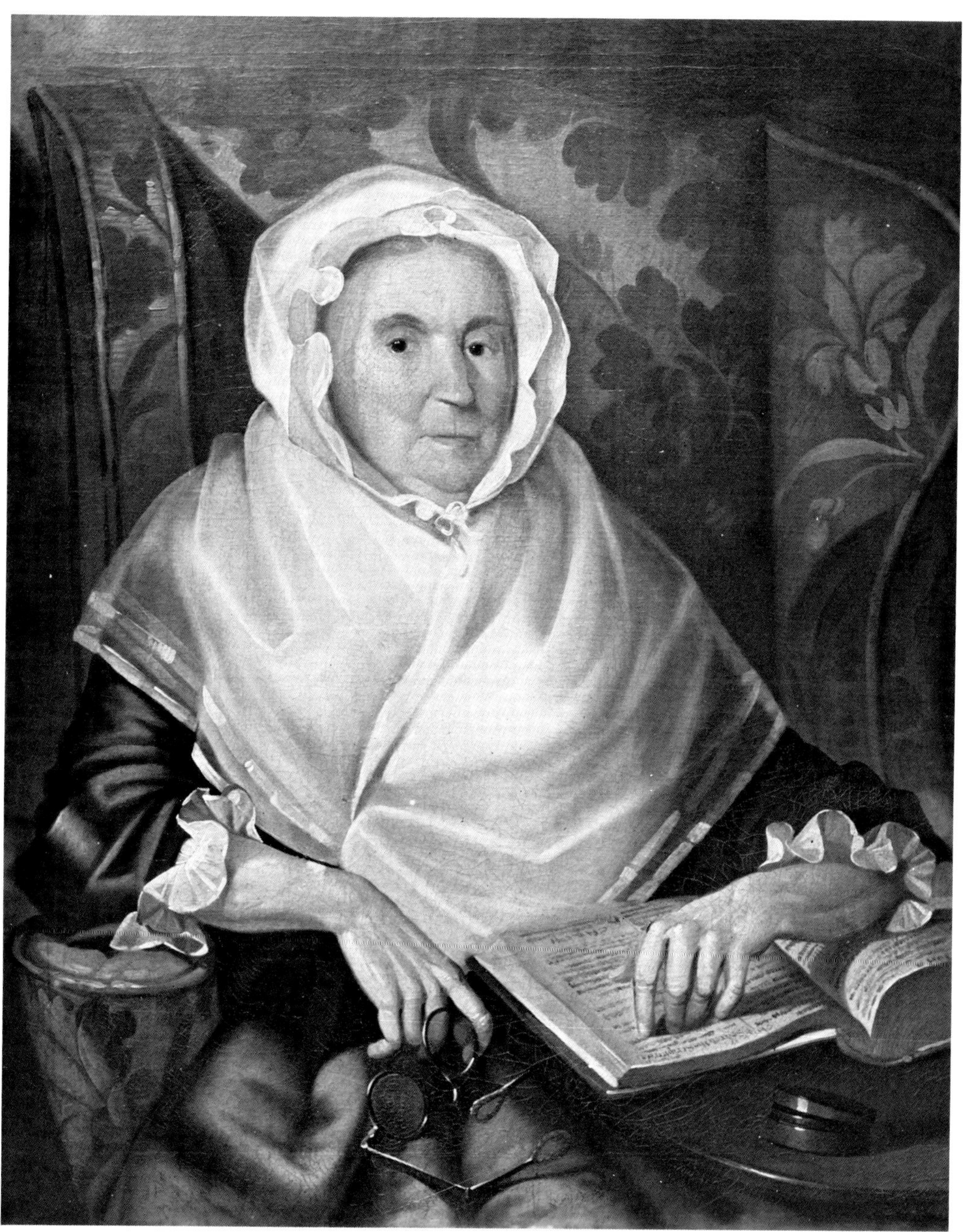

Christian Gullager, American, b. Denmark (1759-1826; lived in America after 1786)

Stephen Salisbury I
Oil on canvas on pulpboard, 1789 (35-5/8 x 28-7/8 in.) Gift of Stephen Salisbury III, 1901.23

This portrait of Stephen Salisbury I (1746-1829) was painted in the spring of 1789 when the sitter invited the Danish-born artist Christian Gullager to visit Worcester. Records indicate that Gullager came from Boston on May 25 and that he stayed for nineteen days. The portrait, as well as likenesses of his mother and of his sister Elizabeth, were painted in Stephen Salisbury's comfortable frame mansion which he built in 1772.

Stephen Salisbury, forty-three when he posed for Gullager, sits easily in a Windsor chair. The work reflects Gullager's professional finish and robust style. Salisbury was born in Boston on September 25,1746. He came to Worcester in 1767 to set up a store in which he sold hardware and a variety of other goods. He married Elizabeth Tucker-man on January 31, 1797. They had three children, but only Stephen Salisbury II survived childhood. A grandchild, Stephen Salisbury III, donor of this portrait, founded the Worcester Art Museum and became the institutions's chief benefactor.

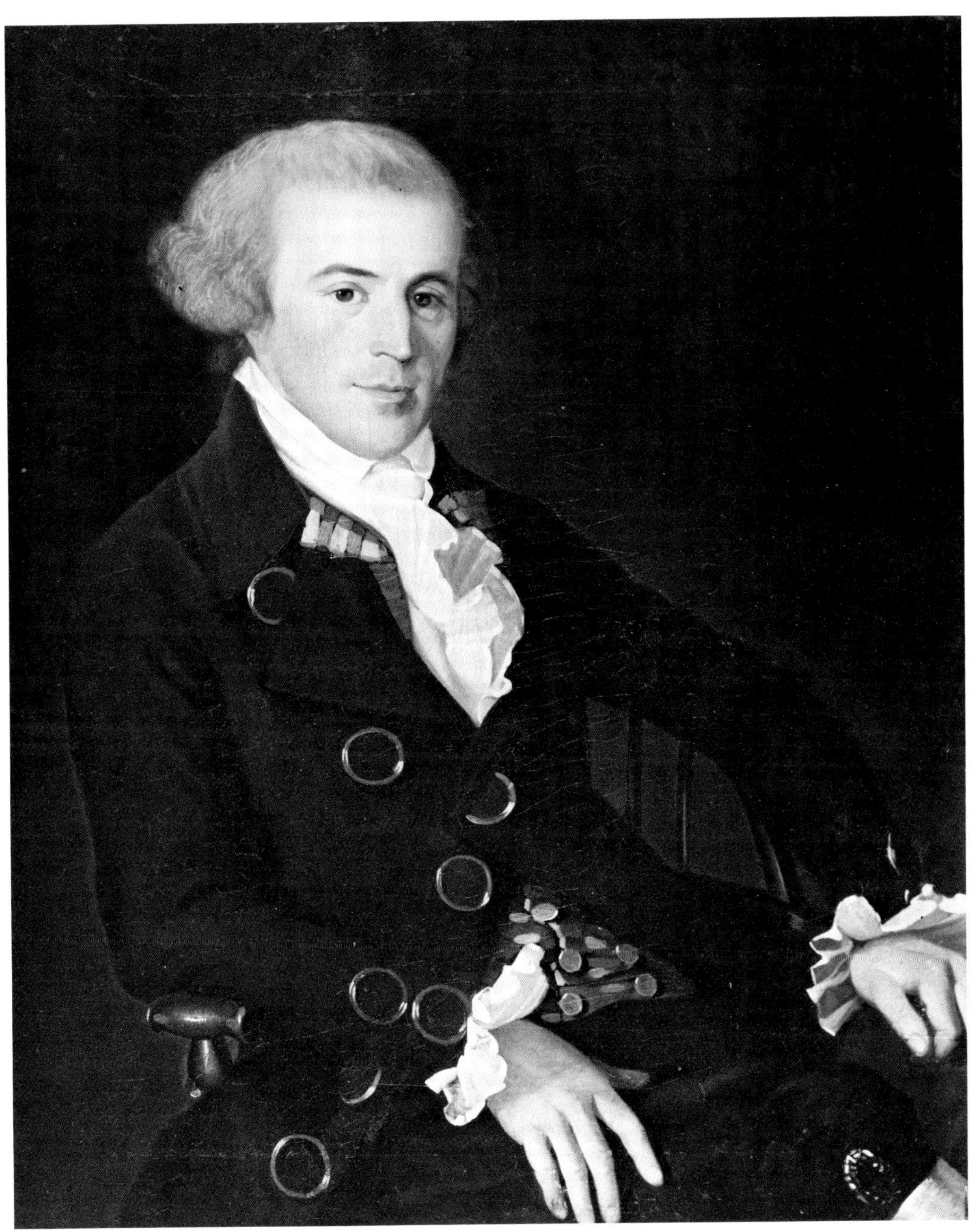

Charles Willson Peale, American (1741-1827)

Charles Pettit
Oil on canvas, 1792 (35-7/8 x 27 in.) Museum purchase, 1919.121

Charles Pettit (1736-1806) was fifty-six when Charles Willson Peale painted his picture in 1792. The work was intended as a wedding present to Pettit's son Andrew. Both the subject and the painter had settled into their post-war pursuits. Charles Pettit, who had served General Washington as assistant quartermaster general of the Continental Army, was well established in the importing business. In his later years, Pettit helped found the Insurance Company of North America. He was also a member of the American Philosophical Society and a trustee of the University of Pennsylvania.

Charles Willson Peale, born in Queen Annes County, Maryland, took up painting after trying his hand as a saddler. He received his first lessons from John Hesselius. In 1767 a group of Maryland citizens sent him to London to study under Benjamin West. After the Revolution, Peale settled in Philadelphia, and in 1786 he opened the Peale Museum where nature specimens were systematically arranged and exhibited. He helped found the Pennsylvania Academy of the Fine Arts. Charles Willson Peale married three times and fathered seventeen children. Five of his sons, Raphaelle, Rembrandt, Rubens, Franklin, and Titian, followed him in pursuit of the arts.

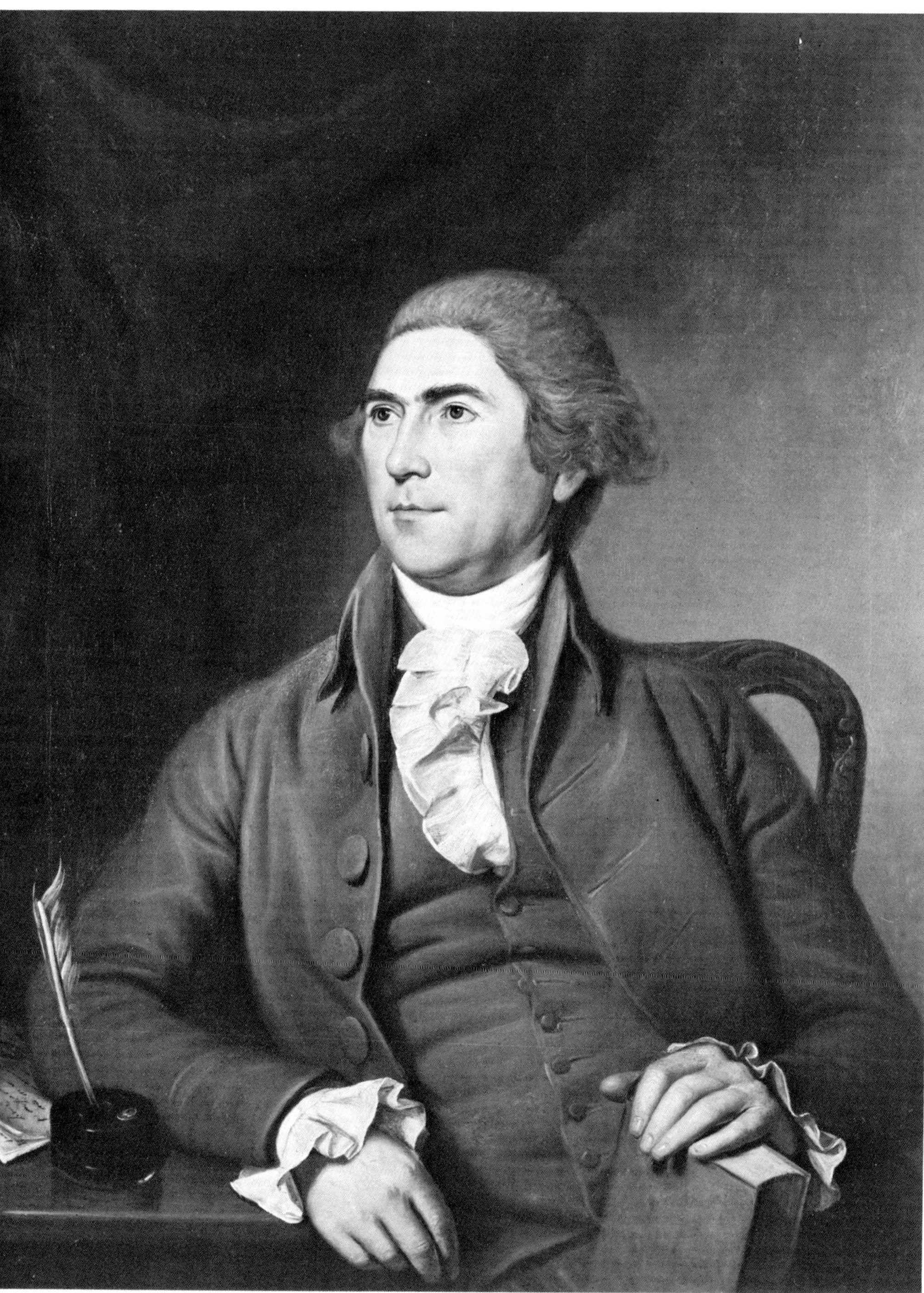

James Earl, American (1761-1796)

Charles Cotesworth Pinckney
Oil on canvas, c. 1795 (35-1/4 x 29-1/8 in.) Museum purchase, 1921.86

Charles Cotesworth Pinckney (1746-1825), who stubbornly yet vainly defended Fort Moultrie and the approaches to Charleston, South Carolina, against the British in 1780, was painted by James Earl approximately fifteen years later. The subject wears the two stars of major general in the South Carolina militia.

The sitter, son of a South Carolina chief justice, studied at Christ Church College, Oxford, and read law at the Middle Temple, London. In the Revolution, he served as an aide to Washington at the battles of Brandywine and Germantown in 1777. Pinckney was a delegate to the Federal Convention which drafted the United States Constitution in 1787. When the French Directory interfered with American commerce on the high seas, President John Adams sent him to Paris in 1797 with John Marshall and Elbridge Gerry to negotiate a settlement of differences. Quasi-war followed after the Americans refused to pay a sum demanded by the Directory as a condition for negotiations.

In his later years, Charles Cotesworth Pinckney was the Federalist candidate for Vice-President in 1800, and he ran against Thomas Jefferson in 1804 and opposed James Madison in 1808 for the Presidency.

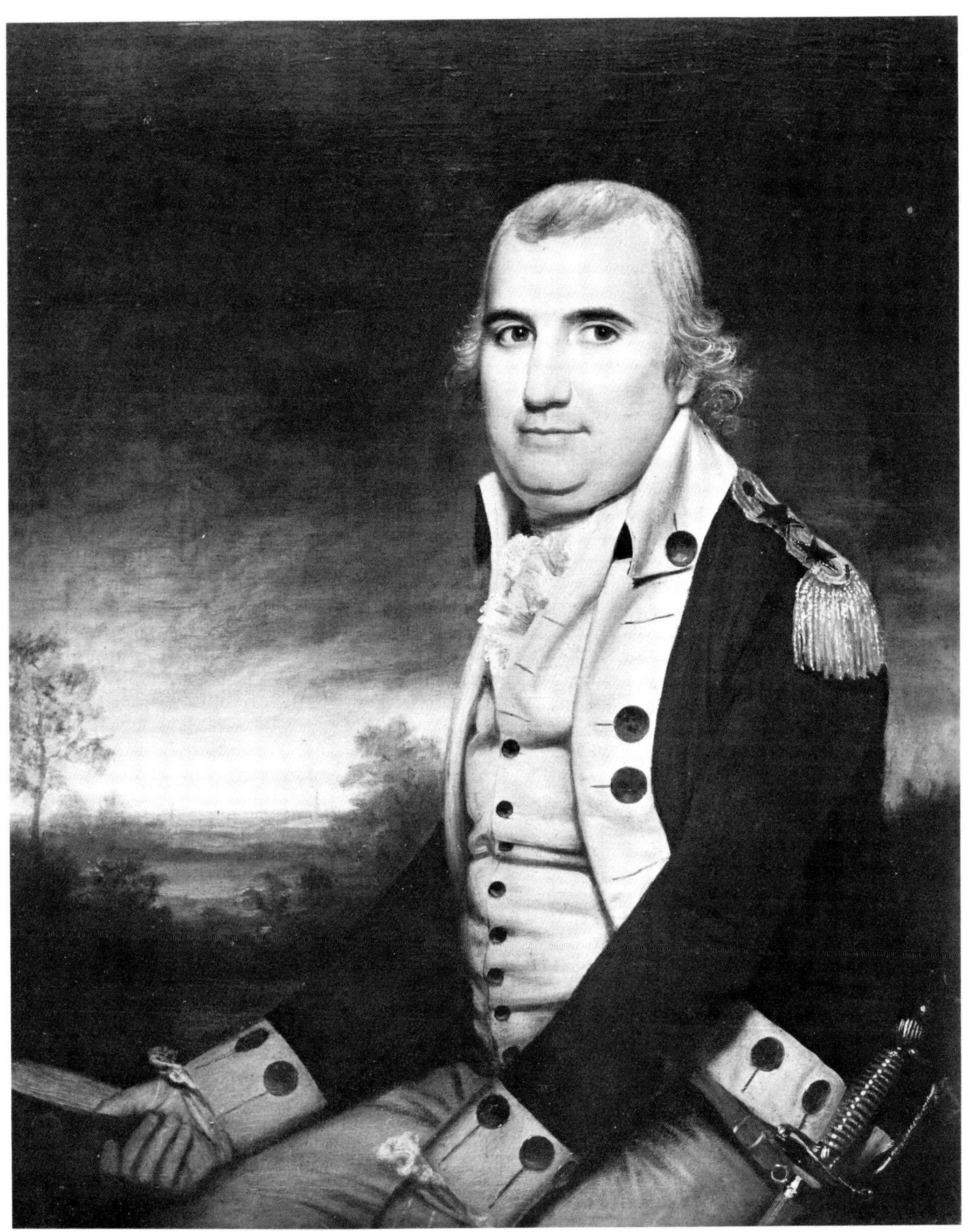

James Sharples, British (c. 1751-1811) or
Ellen Wallace Sharples, British (1769-1849; both active in America
1793-1801 and 1809-1811)

Sarah Fuller Hull
Pastel on paper (9-1/2 x 7-1/2 in.) Alexander and Caroline Murdock DeWitt Fund,
1969.65

General William Hull
Pastel on paper (9-1/2 x 7-1/2 in.) Alexander and Caroline Murdock DeWitt Fund,
1969.64

The portraits of General William Hull and his wife Sarah Fuller Hull
are difficult to date. It would seem that they were executed during the
Sharples' first visit to the United States, between 1793 and 1801,
because William Hull was serving as governor of the Michigan Territory when the British-born artists returned to America in 1809. Form
has been achieved in the portraits by application of color, with little
reliance on the use of line.

William Hull (1753-1825), a native of Derby, Connecticut, was a
graduate of Yale. He served in the Revolution at the battles of White
Plains, Trenton, Princeton, Saratoga, Monmouth, and Stony Point.
When he left the army as a lieutenant colonel in 1781, he took up law
and married Sarah Fuller of Newton, Massachusetts. President Jefferson called on him in 1805 to become governor of the Michigan
Territory, a post he held until the War of 1812. President Madison
appointed him brigadier general on the eve of war and placed him in
command of Michigan forces. William Hull led an invasion of Canada
in 1812, but he was forced back to Detroit when British under Major
General Isaac Brock counterattacked and took our northwestern out-
posts. Hull surrendered Detroit. The campaign was doomed by faulty
planning and by American failure to provide naval power on the Great
Lakes. A court-martial sentenced General Hull to be shot for negli-
gence, but the President spared his life. William Hull and his wife, who
seem to be at ease with the world, are seen in better days in the
Museum's portraits.

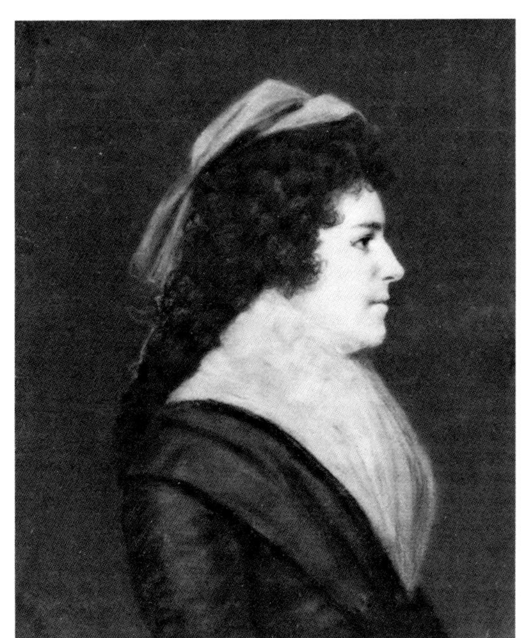 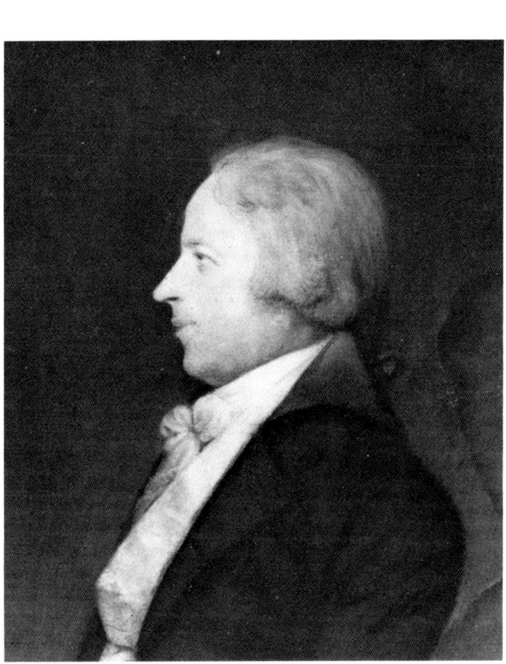

Gilbert Stuart, American (1755-1828; lived in Europe 1775-1792)

Mrs. Perez Morton
Oil on canvas, c. 1802 (29-1/8 x 24-1/8 in.) Gift of the Grandchildren of Joseph Tuckerman, 1899.2

The Worcester Art Museum portrait of Mrs. Perez Morton (1759-1846) was painted approximately seven years after Stuart had established himself at Philadelphia (it was there that he painted his three key portraits of Washington). Among the Museum's works by Stuart, this picture exemplifies best the artist's approach to portraiture. The painter has concentrated on the head and on bringing it to life, while giving less importance to the body and to the clouds in the background. Mrs. Morton, a woman in her forties, has been portrayed as a charming figure possessing depth of mind. She was born Sarah Wentworth Apthorp in Braintree (now Quincy), Massachusetts. Her husband Perez Morton was a well-known Boston lawyer. She was called the "American Sappho" and published in her lifetime various works, including *Quâbi or the Virtues of Nature* (1790); *Beacon Hill* (1797), a patriotic piece; and *My Mind and Its Thoughts* (1823), a volume of prose and poetry. Her brown eyes in Stuart's portrait gaze directly at the spectator as she adjusts her mantilla. The artist originally intended to place her hands in her lap, but he painted out his preliminary drawing when he decided to place her in a more spontaneous pose. Actually an unfinished sketch, the portrait is one of three studies painted of Mrs. Morton during the same year. It was found in Stuart's studio after his death and was purchased in 1862 by Ernest Tuckerman of Newport; the work eventually came into the hands of Stephen Salisbury III, who saw that the picture entered the Museum collection.

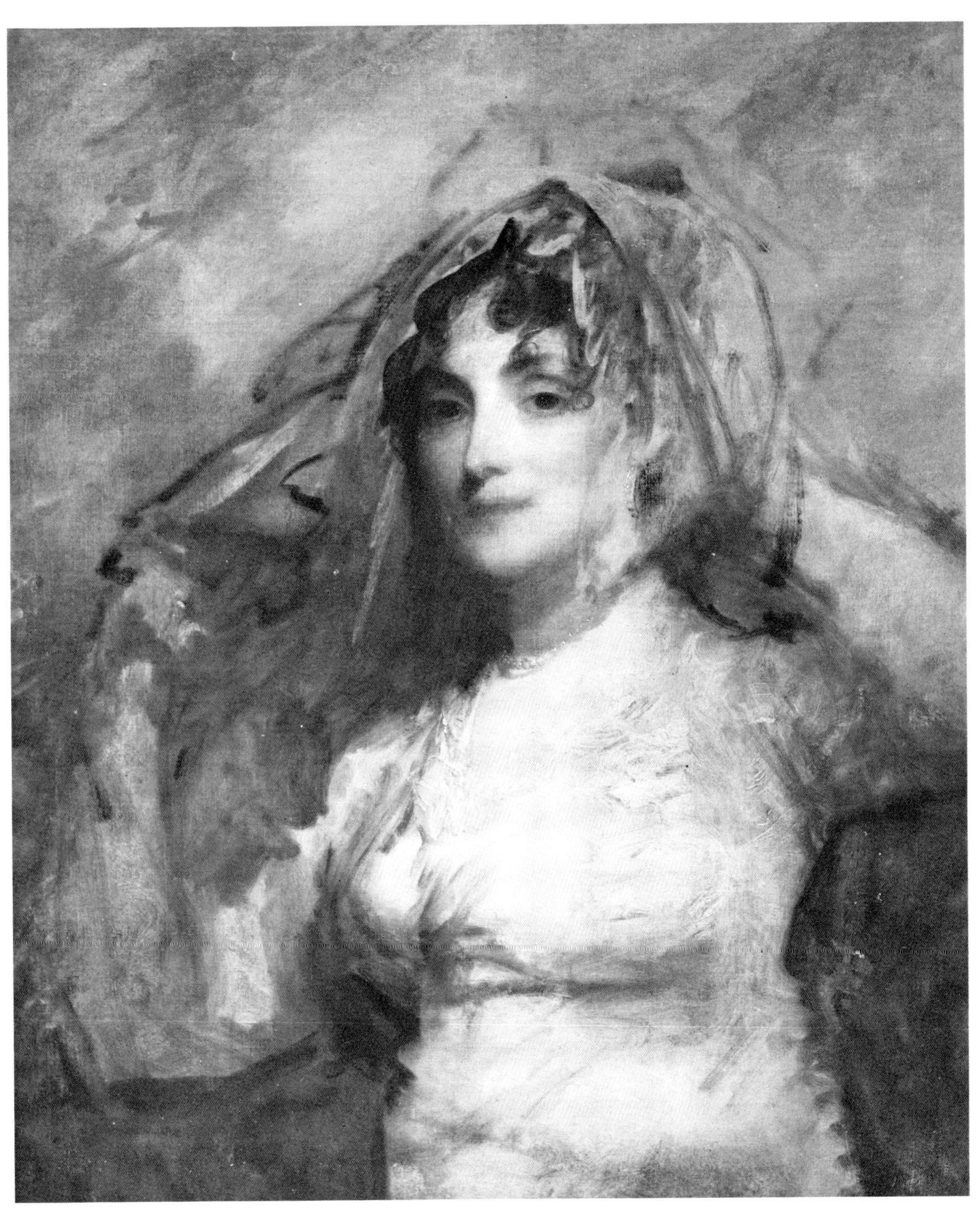

Gilbert Stuart, American (1755-1828; lived in Europe 1775-1792)

Russell Sturgis
Oil on canvas, c. 1820 (30 x 25 in.) Gift of the Paine Charitable Trust, 1965.254

Russell Sturgis (1750-1826) was the son of Thomas and Sarah Paine Sturgis of Barnstable. He became a dealer in hats and furs in Boston. He married Elizabeth Perkins; their daughter, Ann Cushing Sturgis, married Frederick William Paine of Worcester. Sturgis was a close friend of Gilbert Stuart and was painted by him three times. This is the last, and perhaps the best, of those portraits.

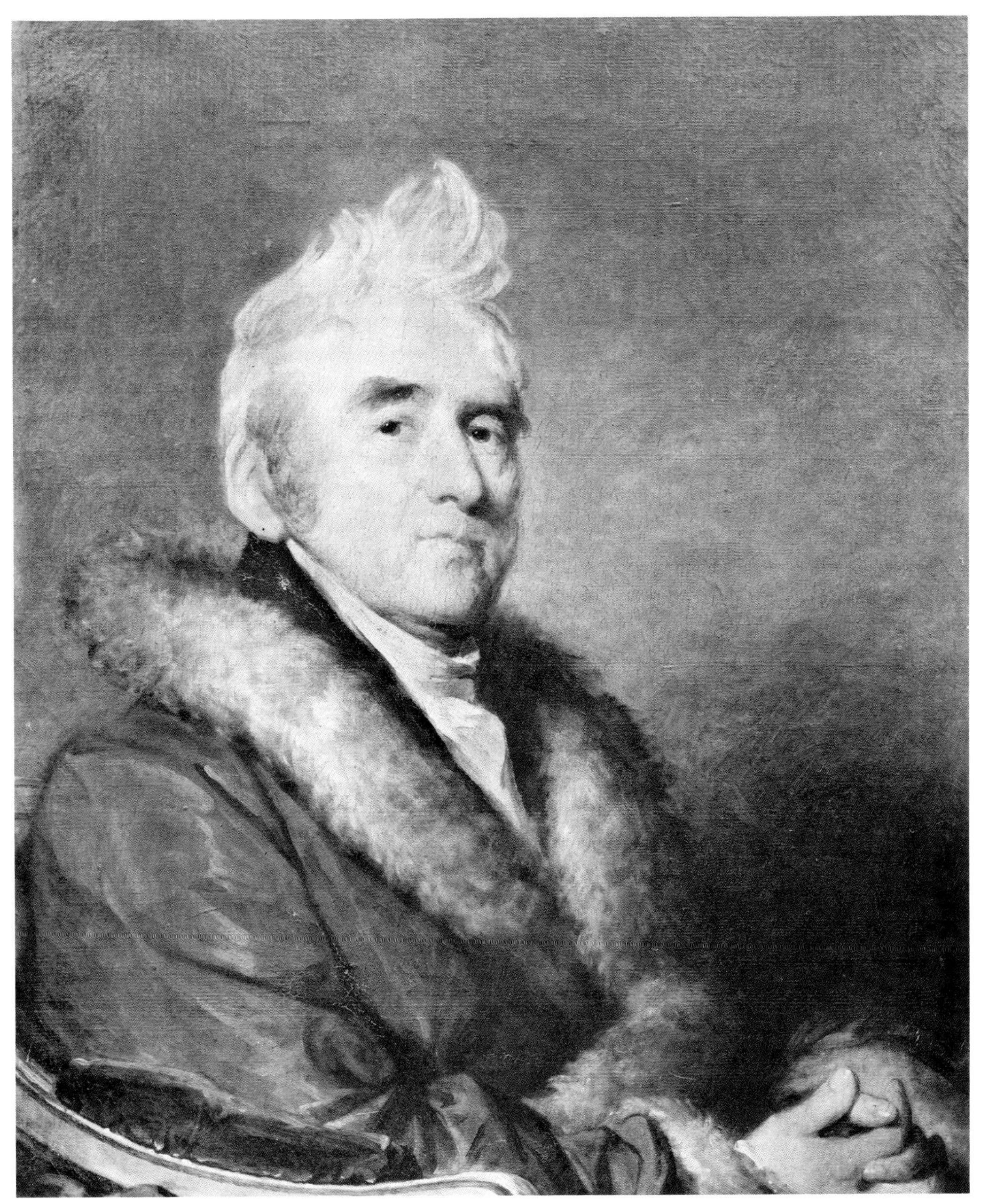

Gilbert Stuart, American (1755-1828; lived in Europe 1775-1792)

Stephen Salisbury I
Oil on canvas, 1823 (28-1/8 x 23-1/4 in.) Gift of Stephen Salisbury III, 1901.32

Christian Gullager had painted Stephen Salisbury in 1789 when he was forty-three. Stephen posed for another portrait late in life before Gilbert Stuart's easel. The sitter, then seventy-six, was an eminently successful Worcester businessman. The portrait of Stephen Salisbury was painted with the sureness and brilliance that only Stuart possessed. The artist showed the effects of old age on the gentleman, and he gave him dignity. Stuart was himself an old man when he painted Stephen Salisbury's portrait.

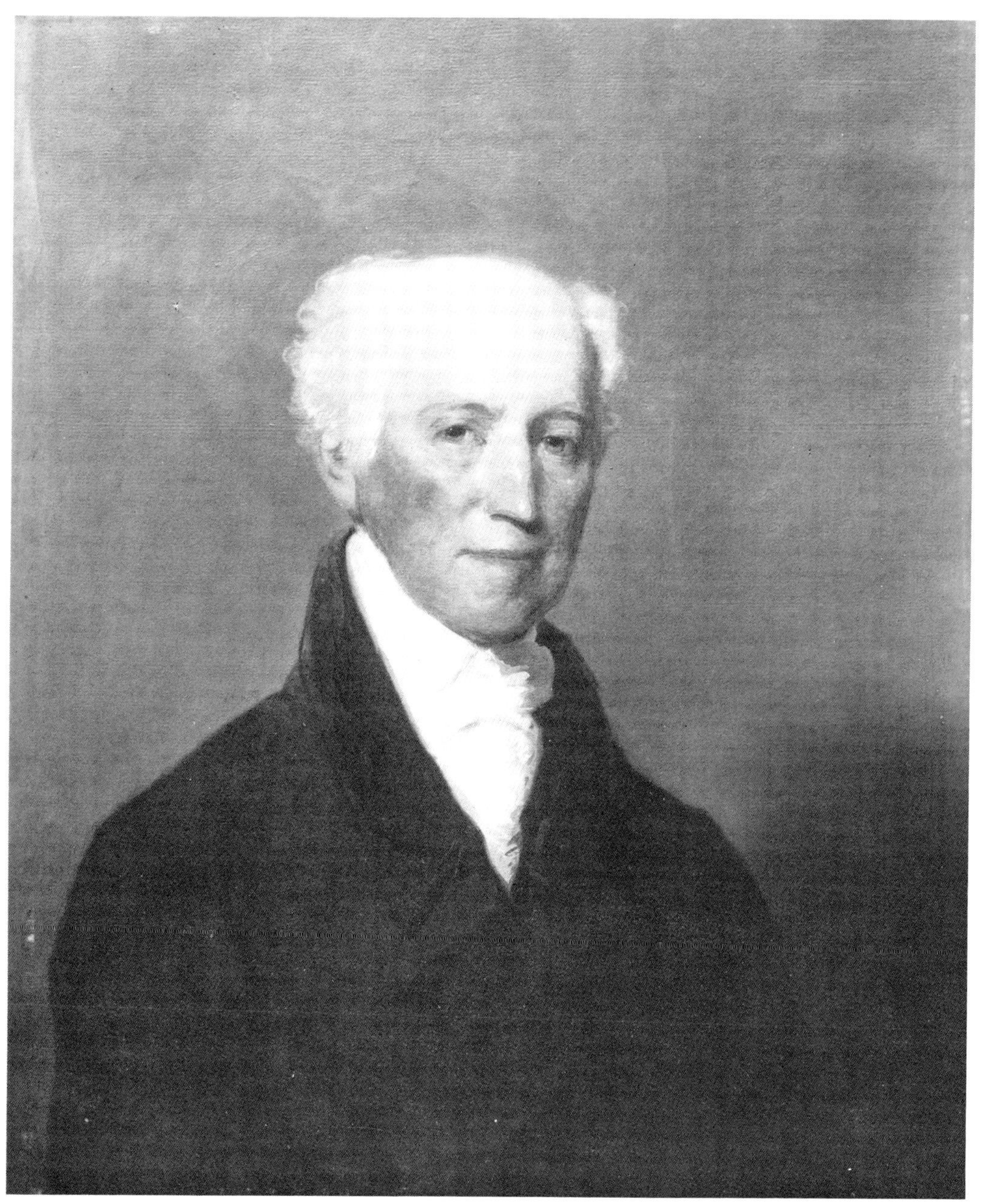

Charles Févret de Saint-Mémin, French (1770-1852; lived in America c. 1793-1810 and 1812-1814)

Thomas Jefferson
Black and white crayon with grayish wash on tinted pink paper, 1804 (23-7/8 x 17 in.)
Museum purchase, 1954.82

Thomas Jefferson (1743-1826), third President of the United States, was nearing the end of his first term in office when he sat before Saint-Mémin's physionotrace apparatus. The President entered in his pocket account book on November 27, 1804, "27, gave St. Menin order on bk. US. for 29.50." The notation covered the purchase of a life-size drawing and forty-eight engravings.

Charles-Balthazar-Julien Févret de Saint-Mémin came from an aristo-cratic family of Dijon, France. At eighteen, he became an ensign in the French Guards, but was compelled to leave the regiment a year later after the Bastille was stormed in 1789. After his family sought refuge in Switzerland, Charles and his father made their way to New York in 1793.

Saint-Mémin turned to his painting hobby to make a living. He devised a physionotrace mechanism (invented by Gilles-Louis Chrétein in 1786) for making accurate, life-size delineations of the head and shoulders, taught himself engraving, and traveled the east coast seek-ing portrait commissions. It was his habit to make a physionotrace drawing first, complete the drawing in crayon, and finally reduce the image through a pantograph to a copper engraving plate. He cus-tomarily made twelve prints from each plate and sold them with the drawing to his patron. Saint-Mémin carried on his portrait work until he returned to France in 1814. He became director of the city museum in Dijon and held the position until his death in 1852.

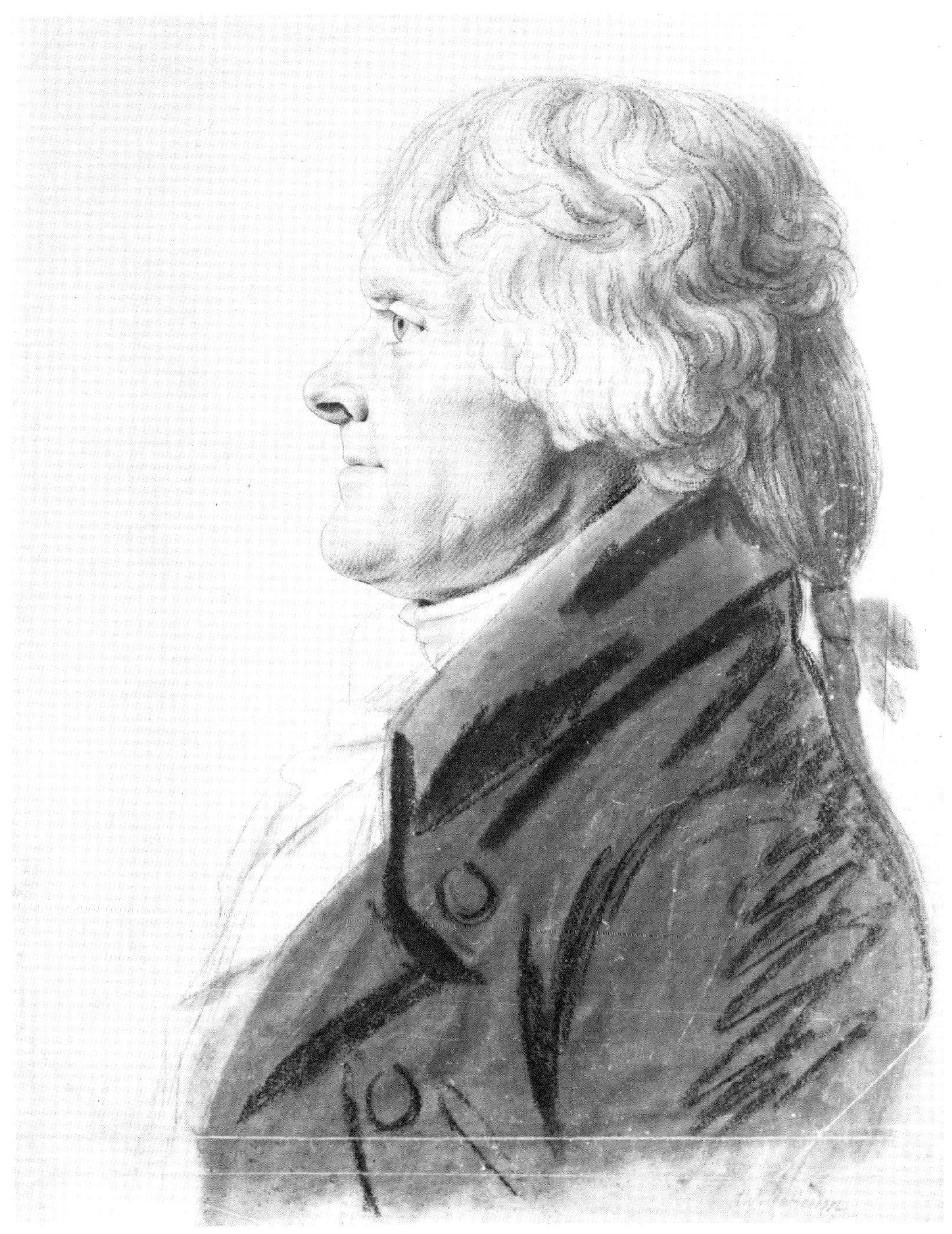

Robert Salmon, British (1775-c. 1845; lived in America after 1828)

Huntress, Wiscasset
Painting on *papier-mâché* tray, 1808 (23-1/8 x 32-3/4 in.) Gift of Lawrence Kendrick Blair
and Colonel John Smith Blair in memory of John S. and Clara Lawrence Blair, 1959.73

The subject of this *papier-mâché* tray is the full-rigged merchant ship
Huntress of Wiscasset. The ship's portrait was executed when the
Huntress probably traded from British ports during Jefferson's em-
bargo in 1808 in order to produce profits for her owner. The inscription "R.S. 1808," at the lower right, indicates that the painting is the
work of Robert Salmon, an outstanding marine artist of Scottish background, who worked at the time in Liverpool, the setting for the
picture. Salmon later emigrated to Boston, Massachusetts, where he
painted with success between 1828 and 1842. His earliest dated work
shows that he was established as a painter by 1800.

In the picture, the *Huntress* is seen under sail in Liverpool harbor. The
docks appear at the right while the shoreline of the Mersey River may
be seen at the left. At the masthead flies a red-bordered pennant,
"Huntress Wiscasset." The rigging has been portrayed in detail, as has
the ship's figurehead, a lively huntress with a bow and arrow. The ship
was under command of Captain John Stinson, who served her owner
Major Robert Elwell of Wiscasset (then part of Massachusetts, now
Maine), a prosperous seaport during the early republic. The *Huntress,*
a vessel of 269 tons, was built in 1804 at Newcastle, eight miles from
Wiscasset.

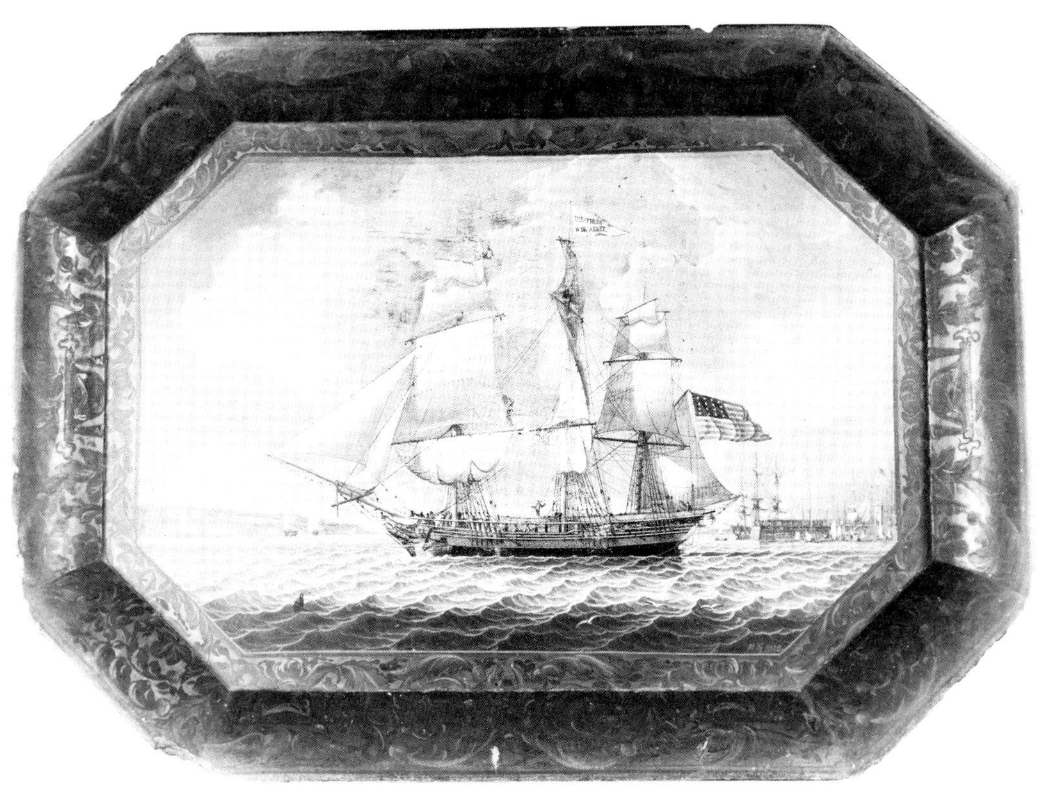

Thomas Sully, American, b. England (1783-1872; lived in America after 1792)

Miss Margaret Siddons
Oil on canvas, 1812 (36-1/8 x 29 in.) Museum purchase, 1917.35

The artist Thomas Sully was sensitive to feminine beauty, which he evoked with sureness in his portraits of ladies. The Museum's painting, *Miss Margaret Siddons,* is no exception. The young woman, conscious of her charm, sits gracefully on a carved and gilded sofa. Beyond her and the billowing curtain stands a classical column, illuminated by the setting sun. The sofa arm, given sculptural form by facile brushwork, casts a strong shadow on the sitter's white Empire gown. The work was executed in 1812, one year after Margaret Siddons of Philadelphia married Benjamin Harbeson Kintzing of the same city. Her sister Mary, a well-known beauty, also posed for the artist in 1812.

Sully settled in Philadelphia about 1808; it was there that he painted a greater part of the twenty-six hundred portraits credited to him. He is famous for his pictures of Lafayette, made during the general's triumphal visit in 1824; of the British actress, Frances Anne Kemble, painted when she played in Philadelphia; and of Queen Victoria, undertaken soon after she ascended Britain's throne. Thomas Sully, born in England, spent his youth in Charleston, South Carolina, where his schoolmate and future miniaturist, Charles Frazer, taught him the rudiments of art. As he advanced in his career, Sully sought and received advice and encouragement from Gilbert Stuart and Benjamin West.

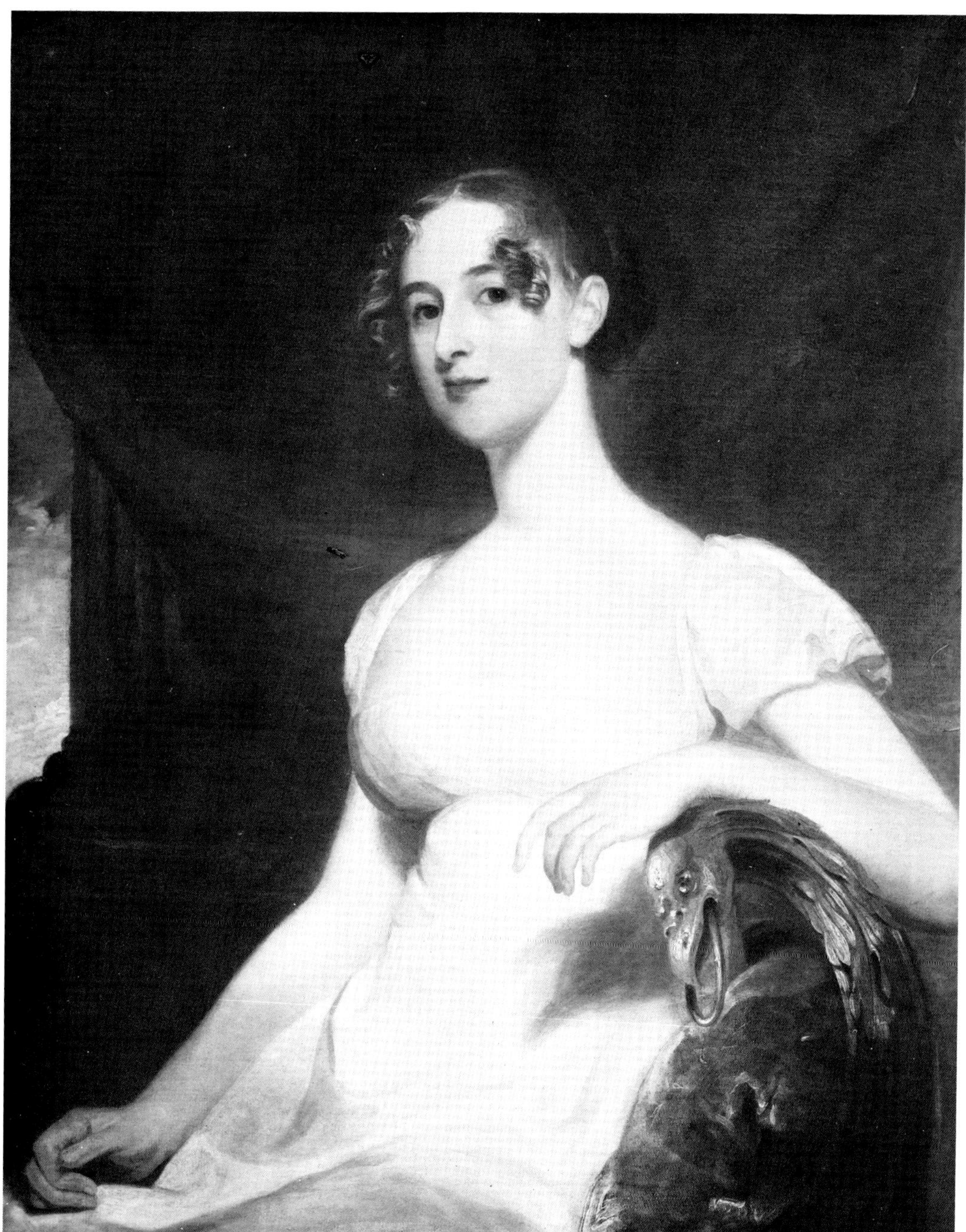

Washington Allston, American (1779-1843)

Christ Healing the Sick
Oil on fiber board, 1813 (28-3/4 x 40-3/8 in.) Museum purchase, 1920.91

Washington Allston, born in South Carolina and graduated from Harvard, began his art studies at the Royal Academy in London, England. During his seven-year stay abroad, he visited the Louvre in Paris and made an extended trip to Italy, where he formed friendships with Samuel T. Coleridge and Washington Irving. After a second stay abroad from 1811 to 1815, he returned to Massachusetts in 1818.

At the beginning of his career, Allston admired the "Grand Manner" of the English school with its emphasis on history painting. Later, he drew on Biblical and literary subjects.

This work, a second study, was painted in 1813 in London. The subject recalls a New Testament text: "When the even was come, they brought unto Him many that were possessed with devils: and He cast out the spirits with His word, and healed all that were sick: . . ." (Matthew 8:16). E.P. Richardson writes about Allston and the picture: "He chose his subjects from the mysterious borderground of miracles like *Christ Healing the Sick* . . . These pictures introduced . . . a brooding note of mystery, a haunting sense of the inner riddle of life, which reminds one of Hawthorne among our romantic writers."

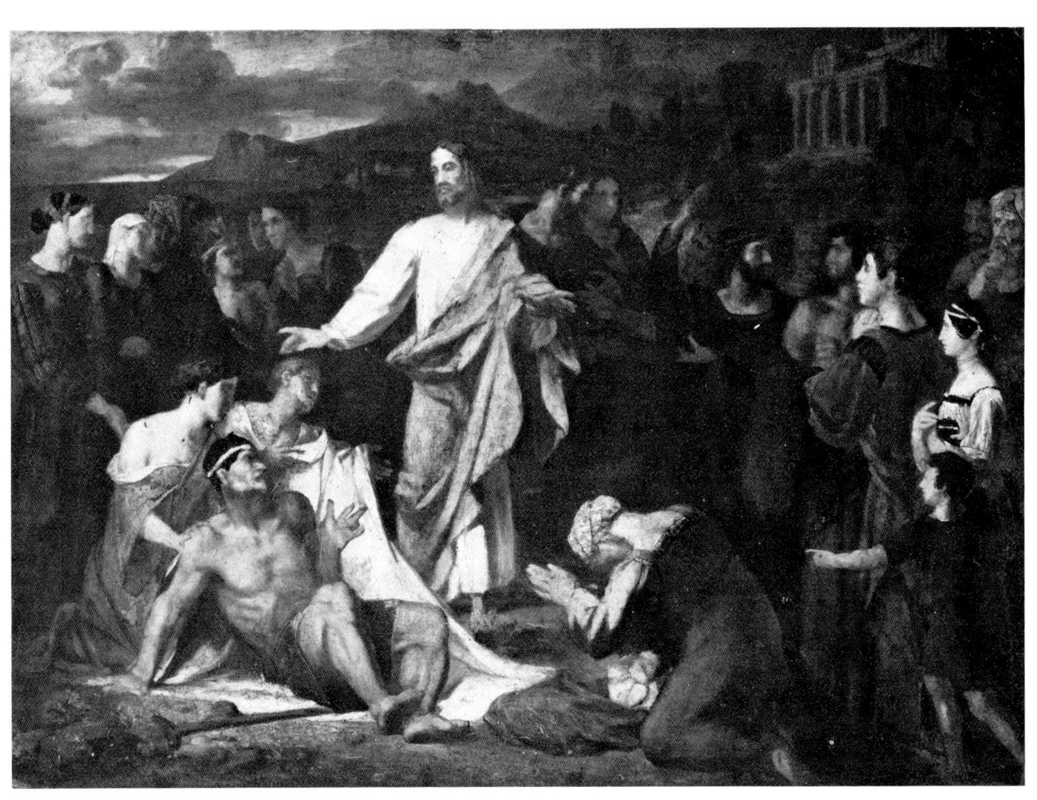

John Ritto Penniman, American (1783-1830/34?)

Edward Tuckerman
Oil on panel, 1823 (9-5/8 x 8 in.) Gift of Stephen Salisbury III, 1899.6

Edward Tuckerman (1740-1818) was a civic leader in Boston. His elder daughter, Elizabeth, married Stephen Salisbury I of Worcester. Their grandson, donor of this portrait, founded the Worcester Art Museum.

John Ritto Penniman made this replica in oil in 1823 from a crayon portrait originally drawn in 1804 by the Dutch-born and Parisian-trained artist Gerritt Schipper (1755-c. 1830). Penniman was active in Boston from about 1805 until the late 1820s. The *Massachusetts Spy* carried an announcement on September 15, 1830, that Penniman had moved from Boston to West Brookfield and that he intended to continue in business—painting military standards, signs, portraits, as well as executing "accurate Drawings of New Inventions designed to be Patented; Original Designs for Diplomas; Vignettes for Bank Bill Engravers; and Designs for Frontispieces and Title Pages of Books." The last public notice about the artist, appearing in *The Rat-Trap* in 1837, told of his agreement to serve for three years as a draughtsman on board the U.S.S. *Independence.*

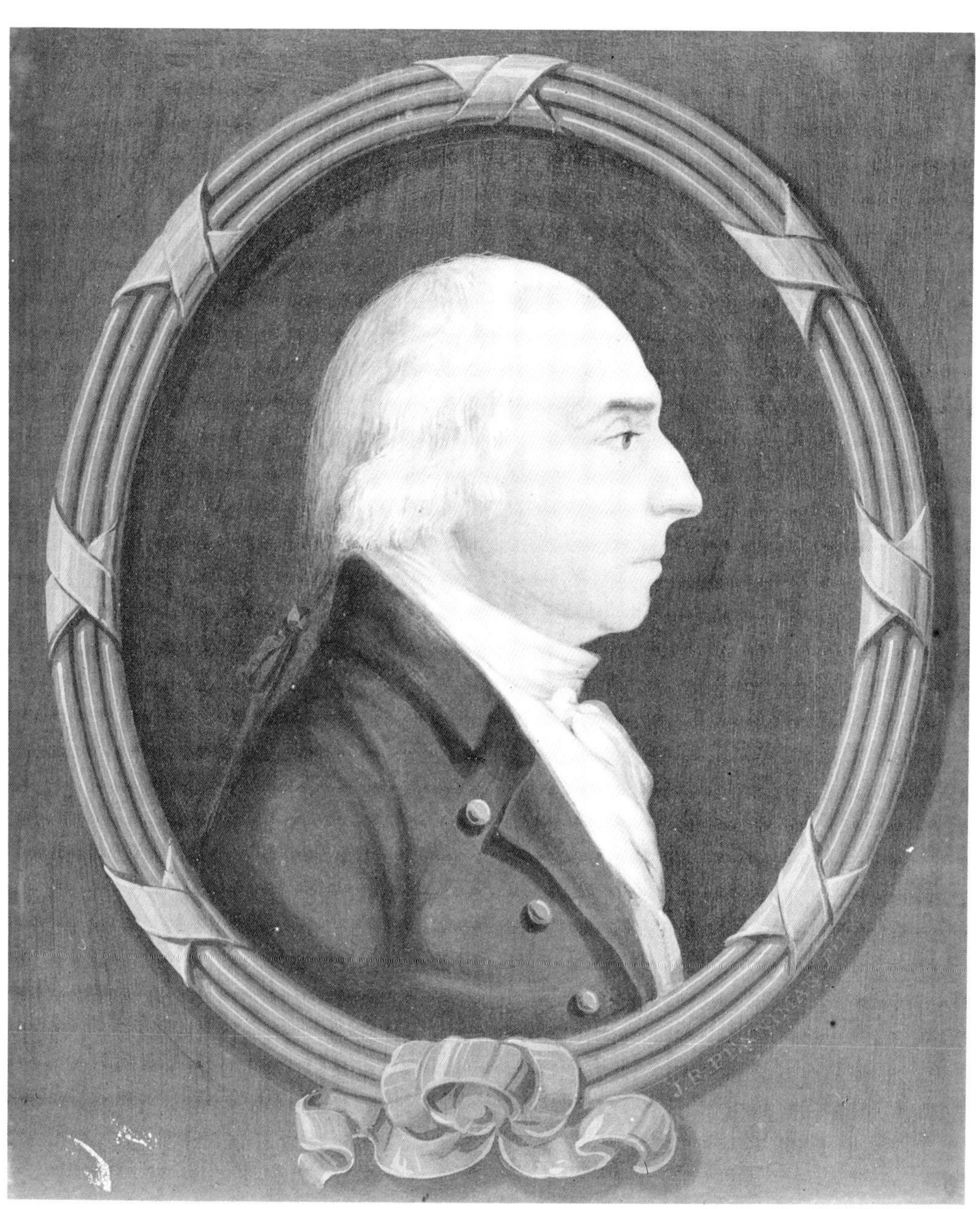

James Frothingham, American (1786-1864)

Jonathan Brooks
Oil on canvas, 1823 (26-1/8 x 21-7/8 in.) Museum purchase, 1918.2

Frothingham was a student and close follower of Gilbert Stuart. He settled in New York in 1826 and enjoyed a successful career as a portraitist.

This painting and its companion were painted in 1823, when Frothingham was still active in Boston and most strongly under Stuart's influence. Jonathan Brooks was a tanner and merchant in Medford, Massachusetts. He is shown at the age of fifty-eight.

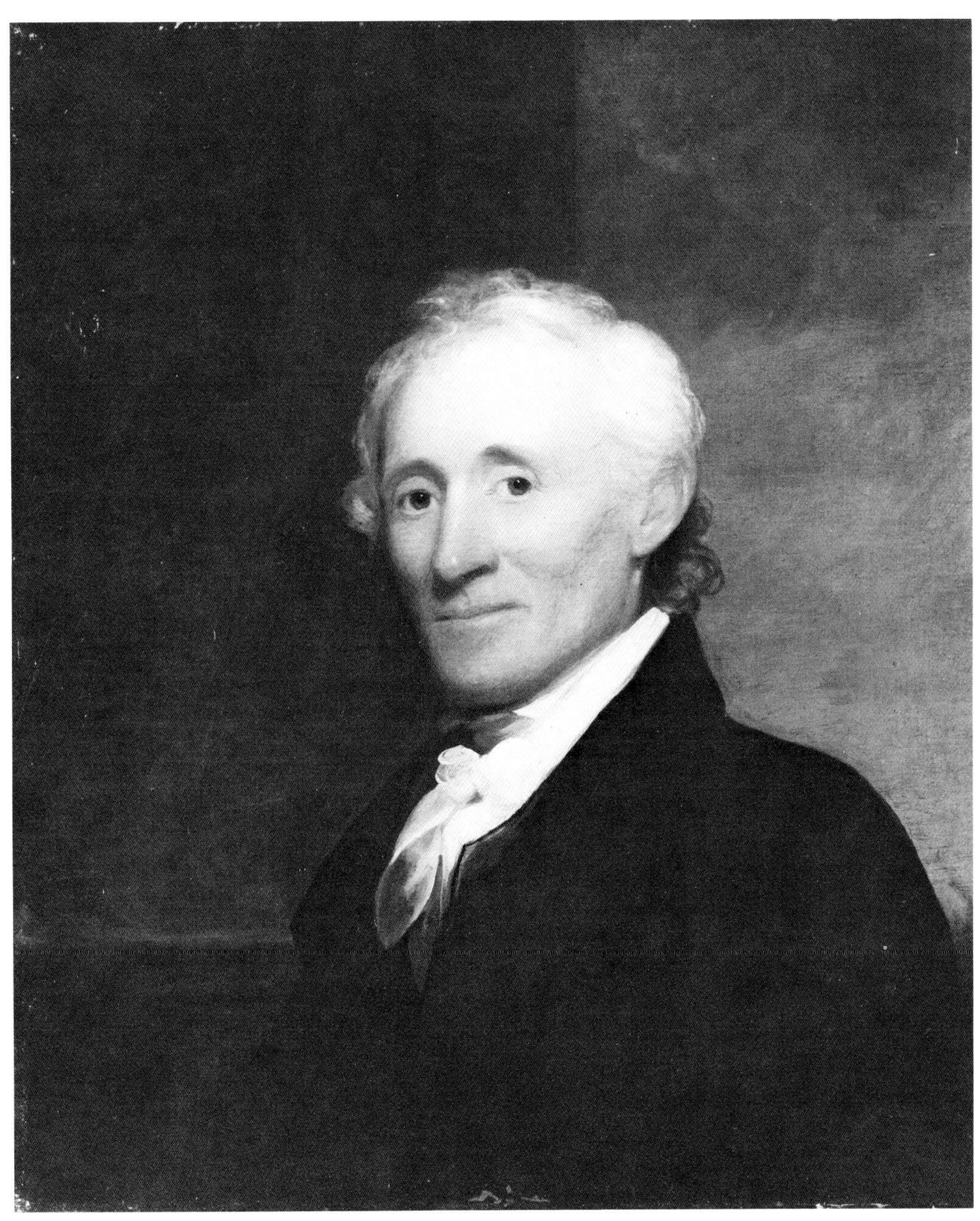

James Peale, American (1749-1831)

Still Life
Oil on panel, 1825 (18-1/2 x 26-5/8 in.) Museum purchase, 1939.37

Still life painting in America appears to have achieved acceptance in the 1820s, though examples of the genre were shown as early as 1795 when James Peale and his nephew Raphaelle Peale sent fruit pieces to the Columbianum exhibition held at Philadelphia.

This work is typical of James Peale's still lifes and is inscribed on the back: "Painted by James Peale/in the 76 year of his age 1825." The subject matter, illuminated by overhead light, is given substance and form in the dark atmosphere. The artist has taken pleasure in painting the details, including a variety of fruit and the richly decorated Chinese export dish. Following the Dutch tradition, the artist has painted the table edge in shadow and has placed it parallel to the edge of the picture.

James Peale began his painting career by assisting his elder brother, Charles Willson Peale. During the Revolution, James was an officer of the Maryland Line. After war service, he joined his brother at Philadelphia, where they decided in 1786 to divide their portrait work — Charles to paint canvases and James to specialize in miniatures. James followed his chosen field until failing eyesight compelled him to work in a larger format; he, therefore, turned to still life about 1820. The artist in his old age showed his adaptability by taking up a new form in which he excelled.

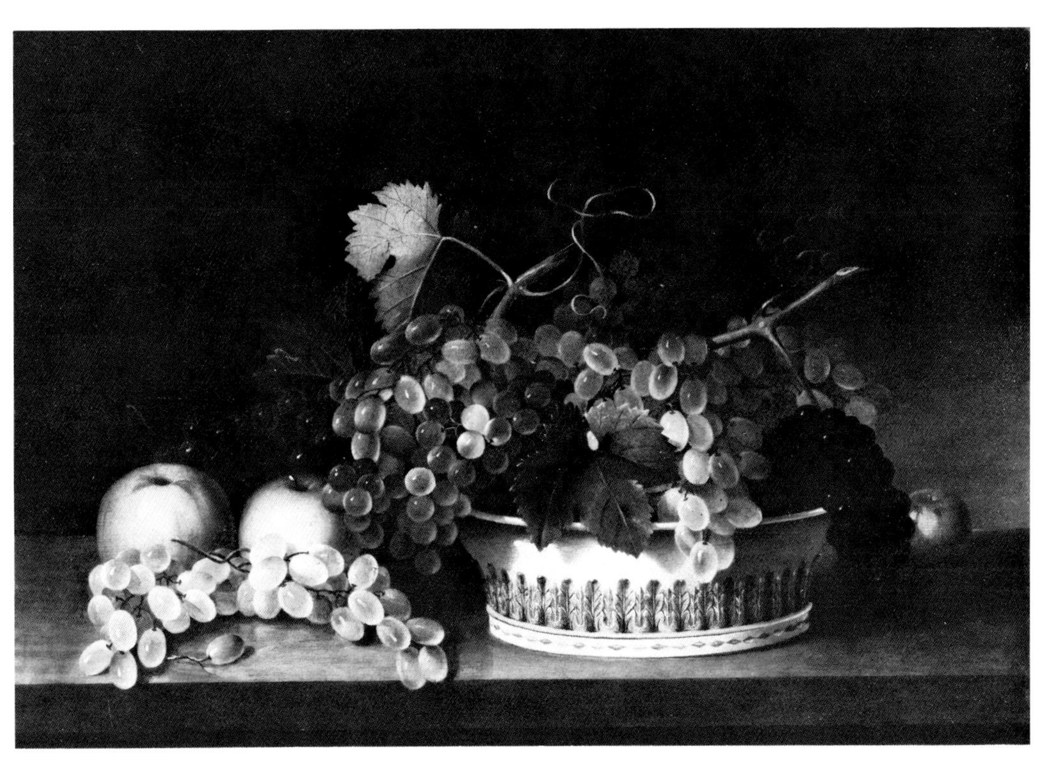

Attributed to William Dunlap, American (1766-1839)

Portrait of George Spalding
Oil on canvas, 1826? (30-1/8 x 25-1/8 in.) Museum purchase, 1917.1

William Dunlap stands as a singular figure in the early history of the American republic. He is best known for his two-volume work, *The History of the Rise and Progress of the Arts of Design in the United States,* published in 1834, in which he surveyed the development of the fine arts in America. This work is still useful to art historians as it contains over two hundred critical biographies of the nation's first painters, printmakers, and sculptors.

A native of Perth Amboy, New Jersey, William Dunlap showed an aptitude for art in his youth, in spite of losing the use of his right eye in a boyhood accident. When he was eighteen, he went to London to study painting for three years under the American expatriate Benjamin West. Upon his return to the United States in 1787, Dunlap established himself as a portrait painter in New York City. During his long life, he also pursued careers in writing, theater management, and miniature painting. In 1826 he helped found the National Academy of Design and later became a vice-president of the institution.

When this painting was acquired in 1917 from the New York dealer William Macbeth, it entered the collection as a portrait of George Spalding. The sitter was subsequently described in the Worcester Art Museum *Bulletin* as a "young man, who is believed to have been of a prominent New York family." The canvas has an inscription on the reverse: "W. Dunlap/N. Y. 1826," but scholars do not accept it as Dunlap's hand. The work, however, has remained associated with Dunlap since the subject is similar in visual qualities to known pictures by the artist.

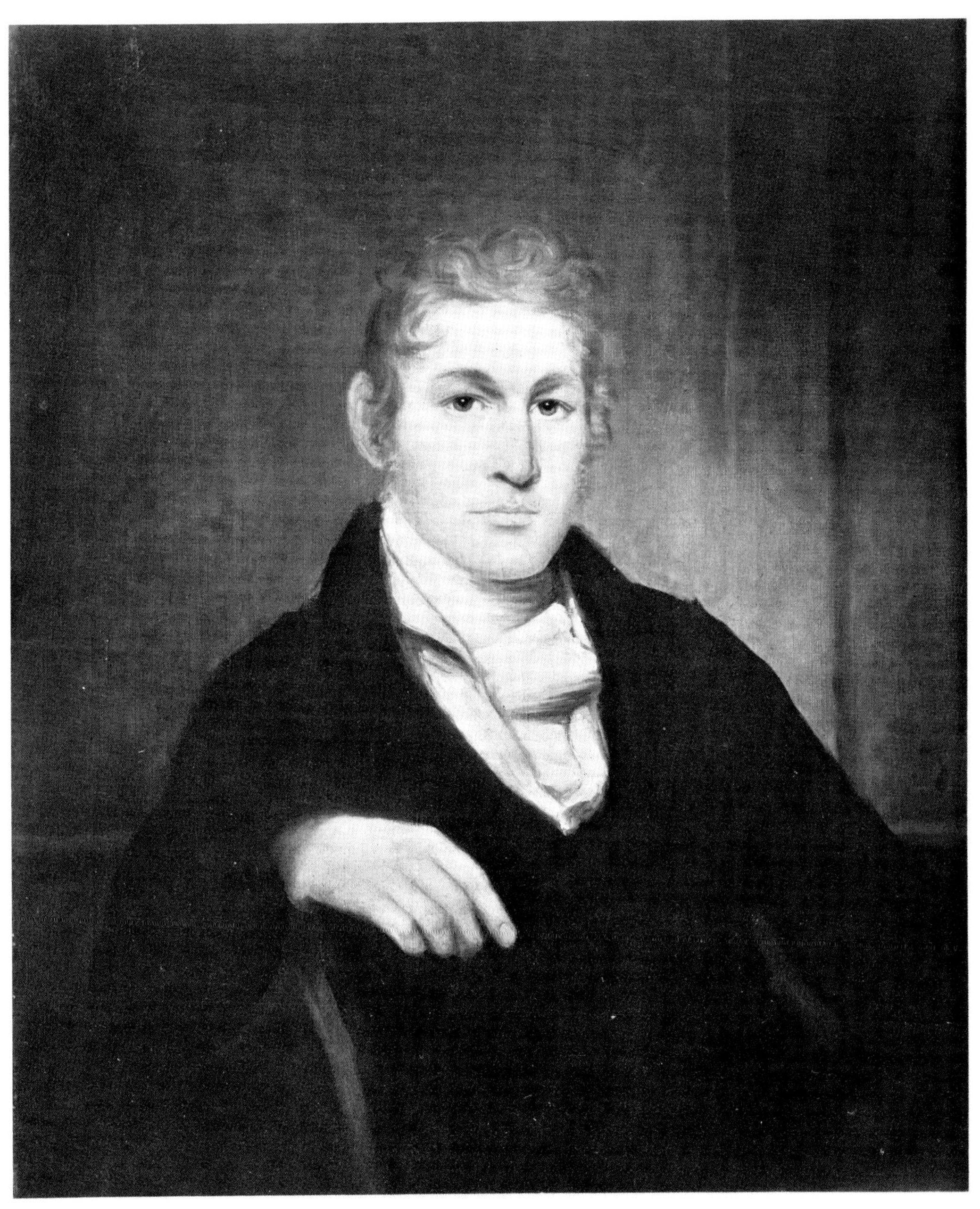

Chester Harding, American (1792-1866)

Stephen Salisbury II
Oil on canvas, 1829 (29-7/8 x 24-7/8 in.) Bequest of Stephen Salisbury III, 1907.109

Chester Harding was a self-taught portrait painter who was born in Conway, Massachusetts. He worked at many trades before turning to painting and then worked his way from the status of an itinerant portraitist to become one of the most successful painters in New England. He emulated Stuart in manner and succeeded him as a fashionable portraitist in Boston.

Stephen Salisbury II was thirty-one when Harding came to Worcester in 1829 to paint his portrait. He had graduated from Harvard in 1817 where he began to study law, and was about to depart for a European tour. He lived to be eighty-six and was a leading figure in Worcester.

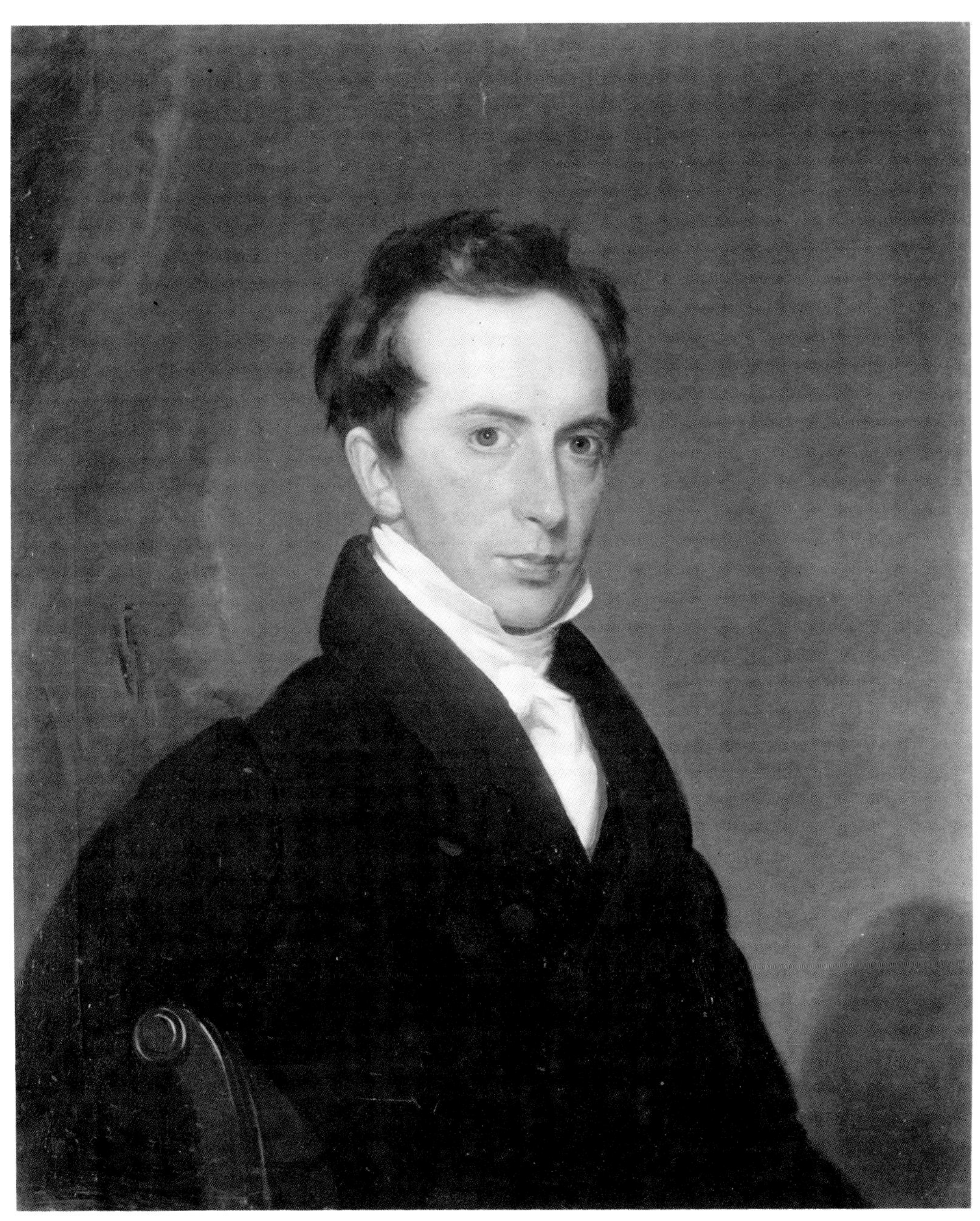

Chester Harding, American (1792-1866)

Mrs. Stephen Salisbury I (Elizabeth Tuckerman)
Oil on canvas, 1829 (30-1/8 x 25 in.) Bequest of Stephen Salisbury III, 1907.32

When Harding came to Worcester in 1829 to paint the Salisbury portraits, he had recently returned from Europe to take up residence in Boston. He was enjoying great popularity as a fashionable portraitist.

It is interesting to compare this portrait of Mrs. Salisbury at age sixty-one with Gilbert Stuart's portrait of her almost twenty years earlier. It is recorded that Mrs. Salisbury was displeased with Harding's likeness, thinking it unflattering, yet in many ways she seems more approachable here than in Stuart's sparkling but rather forbidding image.

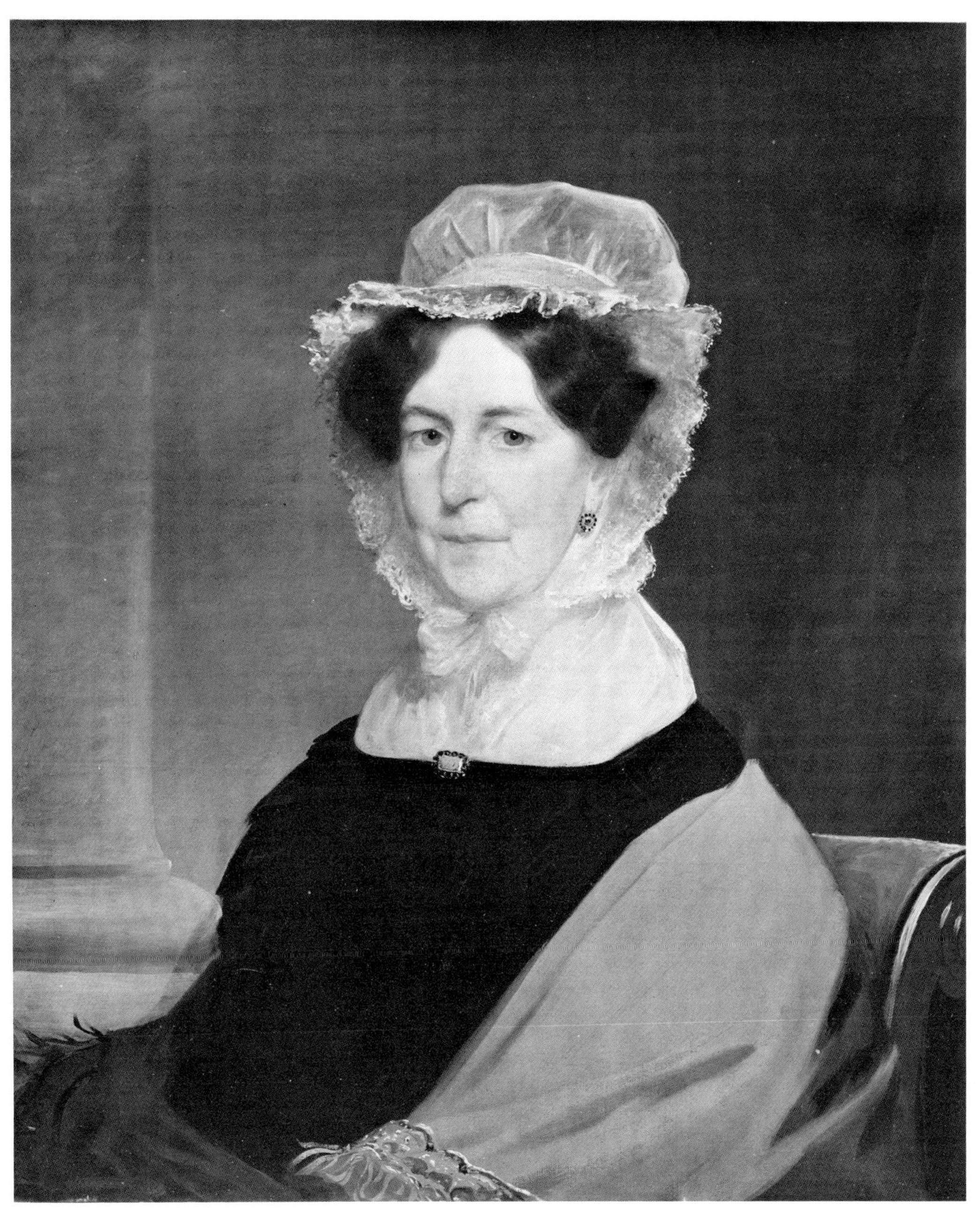

Alvan Fisher, American (1792-1863)

Saturday Afternoon
Oil on canvas, late 1820s (30 x 25 in.) Bequest of Dwight Dunn, 1913.91

Alvan Fisher, a native of Needham, Massachusetts, learned painting from a mediocre Boston artist and began his career as a portrait painter. His draughtsmanship always remained primitive and his portraits are undistinguished, but as early as 1811 he began to paint landscapes and genre scenes. *Saturday Afternoon,* painted in the late 1820s, is a good example of Fisher's genre painting; the figures are clumsily drawn and somewhat stiffly posed, but these young people amusing themselves in a hay barn are presented realistically and without artificial sentimentality.

In taking up genre painting, Fisher became a pioneer in one of the most popular fields of American nineteenth-century painting, though unfortunately it is not a field well represented in the Worcester Art Museum. Paintings of ordinary people, especially Americans, at work and play were well suited to the increasing emphasis on democracy and nationalism in American popular culture. Not only were paintings of this type successful at exhibitions and sales; they were also fre-quently reproduced in prints and thus became available to an audi-ence which would never have been able to afford the originals.

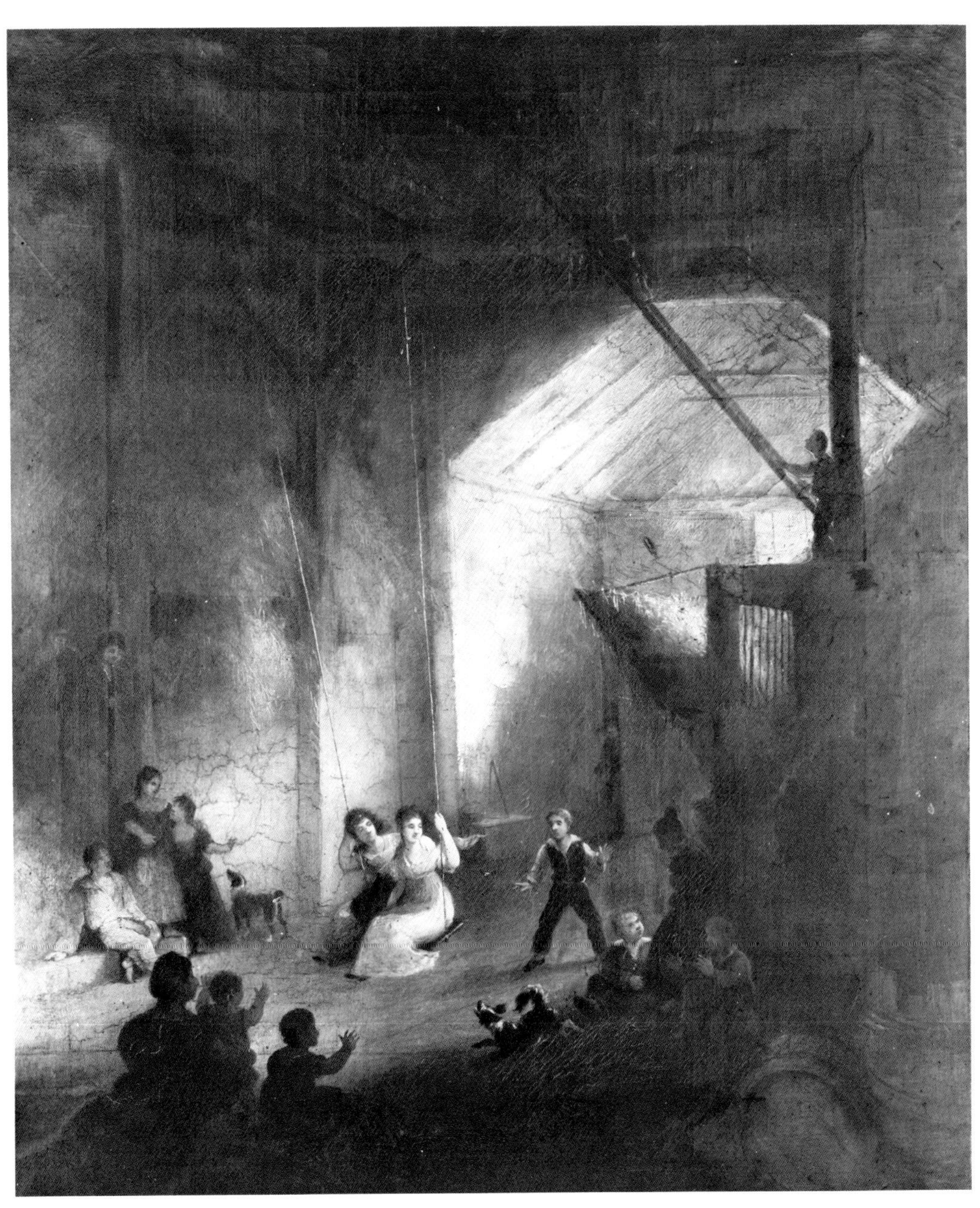

Samuel Finley Breese Morse, American (1791-1872; lived in Europe 1811-1815 and 1829-1833)

Chapel of the Virgin at Subiaco
Oil on canvas, 1830-1831 (30 x 37 in.) Bequest of Stephen Salisbury III, 1907.35

Morse was a leading exponent of academic Romanticism in America after his student years in London between 1811 and 1815. He was a founder of the National Academy of Design and had a successful painting practice. He became discouraged with the American taste, however, and gave up painting in 1845. His later achievements include the invention of the telegraph.

This highly romantic landscape was painted in Rome for Morse's friend and patron Stephen Salisbury II. Morse himself chose the subject, from the oil sketch he had made on the site. He reported to Salisbury: "... I can truly say, I have painted it *con amore,* and that I esteem it myself the *best landscape* I ever painted."

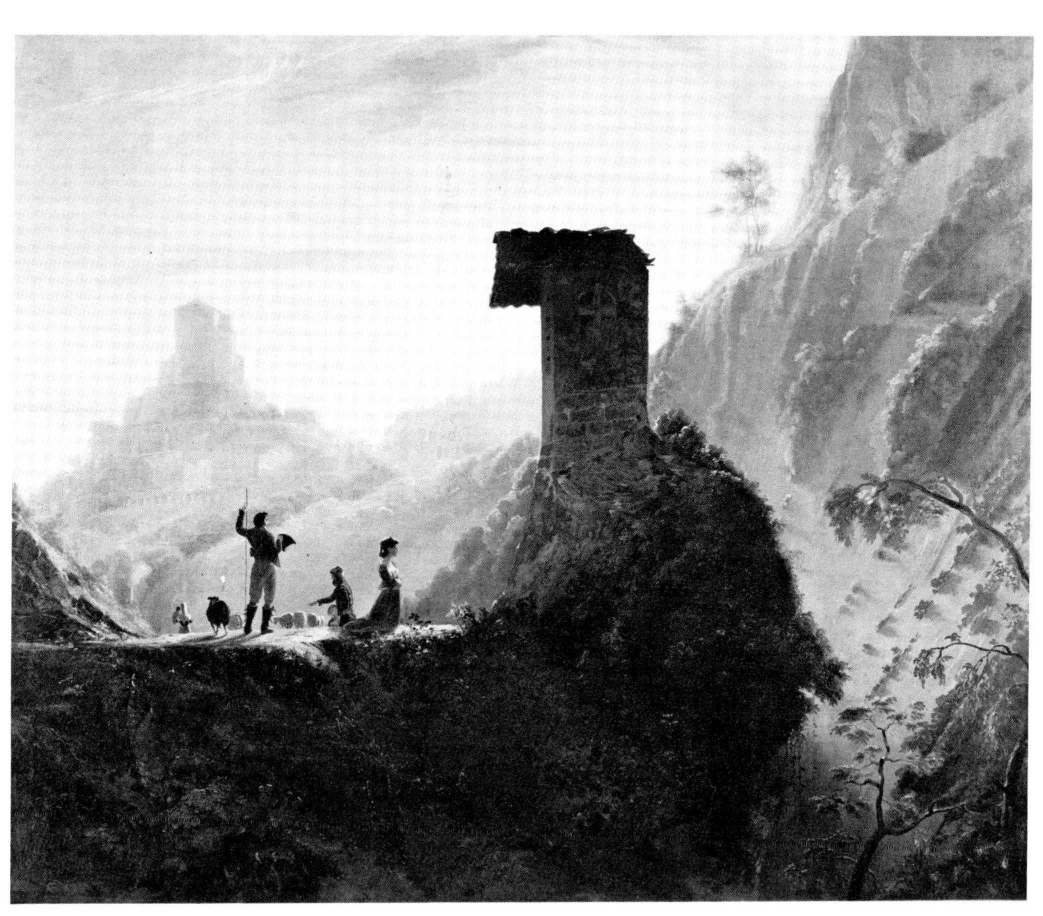

Thomas Doughty, American (1793-1856)

View of Swampscott, Massachusetts
Oil on canvas, 1837? (32-1/4 x 48-1/4 in.) Museum purchase, 1946.35

A self-taught painter, Doughty was a pioneer in developing a truly native style of American landscape painting. Although he was never formally allied with the Hudson River School, his name is often connected with the group. He shared their conception of landscape, minute in detail yet panoramic in scale.

This painting was probably done while Doughty was living in Boston. The date of 1837 is traditionally associated with it. It was purchased from the artist by Charles A. Stetson of New York and Swampscott, a prominent art collector and proprietor of the Astor House in New York.

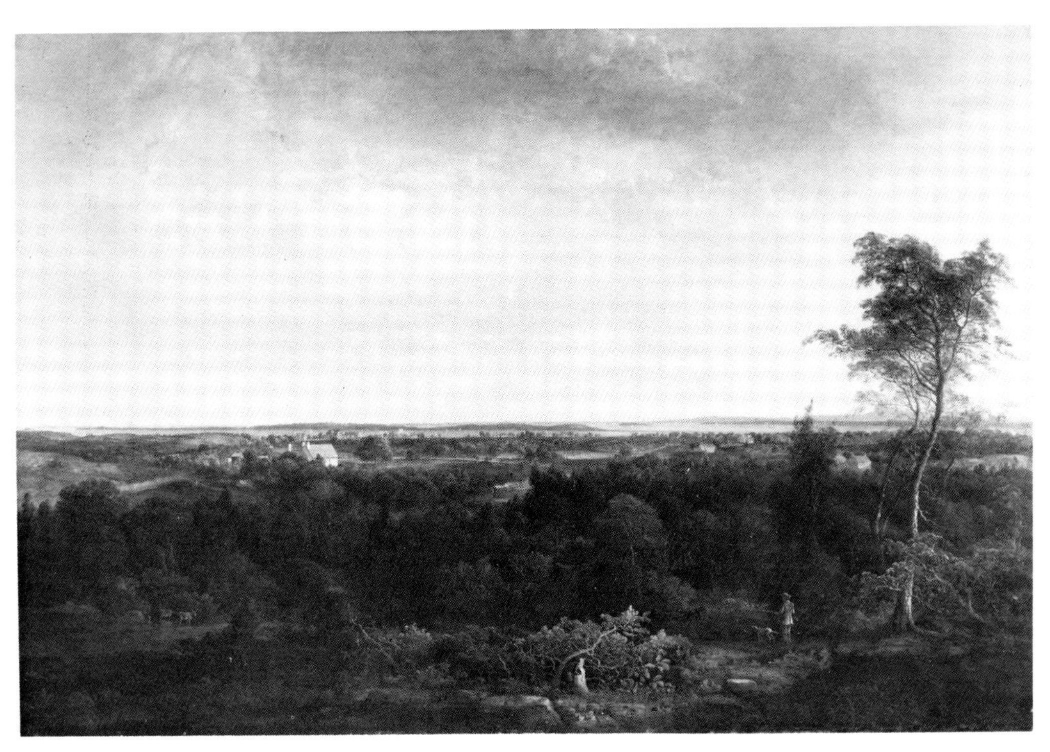

Erastus Salisbury Field, American (1805-1900)

Eleazar Cowles
Oil on canvas, 1837 (30-1/4 x 26-1/8 in.) Museum purchase, 1975.81

Itinerant folk artists, such as Erastus Salisbury Field, at work just before the invention of photography in 1839, found a considerable market for their likenesses among the more prosperous citizens of New England. These nonacademic artists or limners often came to their art by way of a craft. They might begin as house painters, drum or sign painters, cabinetmakers, or carvers of ship figureheads.

As a young man, having already painted several portraits, the itinerant Erastus Field from Leverett, Massachusetts, had the unique opportunity to work in the New York studio of the painter and inventive genius Samuel F. B. Morse. Even though Field's training as a painter lasted only three months, it modified to some extent the technique and style of his early portraits, especially the subject's pose and the smooth manipulation of paint.

In 1837 at the height of his profitable career as a portrait painter, Field limned the faces of numerous Amherst residents, among them these striking delineations of his friends and neighbors, the Cowles family. Despite their very similar stylization, each character emerges strikingly with his own strong individual personality.

Only a few years after these portraits were painted, the daguerreotype was introduced to America by his former teacher, Morse, and Field's portrait commissions from rural patrons began to dwindle. During the second part of his long career, Field painted his own versions of Biblical and historical scenes.

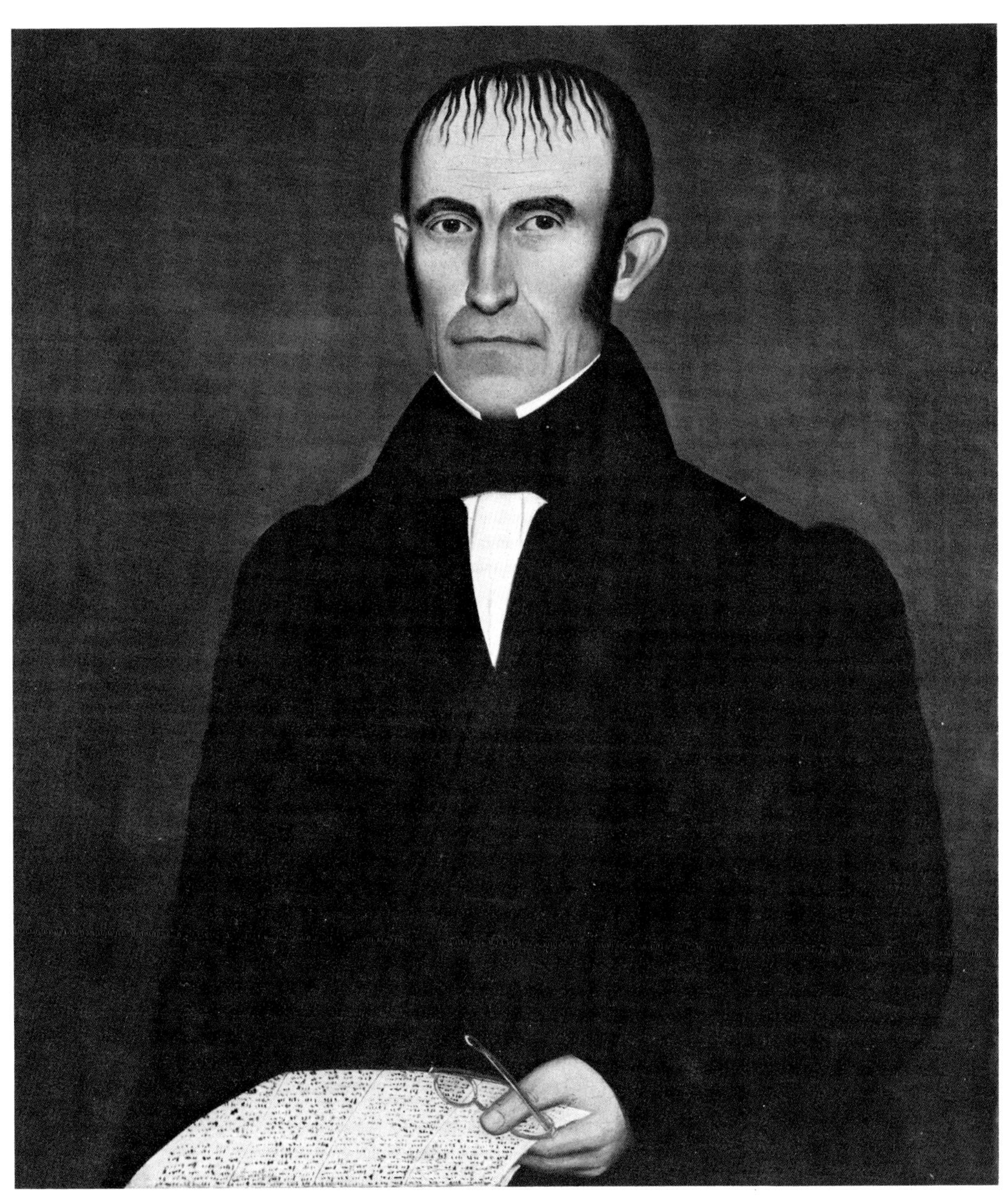

Erastus Salisbury Field, American (1805-1900)

Sibbel Montague Cowles
Oil on canvas, 1837 (30-1/4 x 26-1/4 in.) Museum purchase, 1975.82

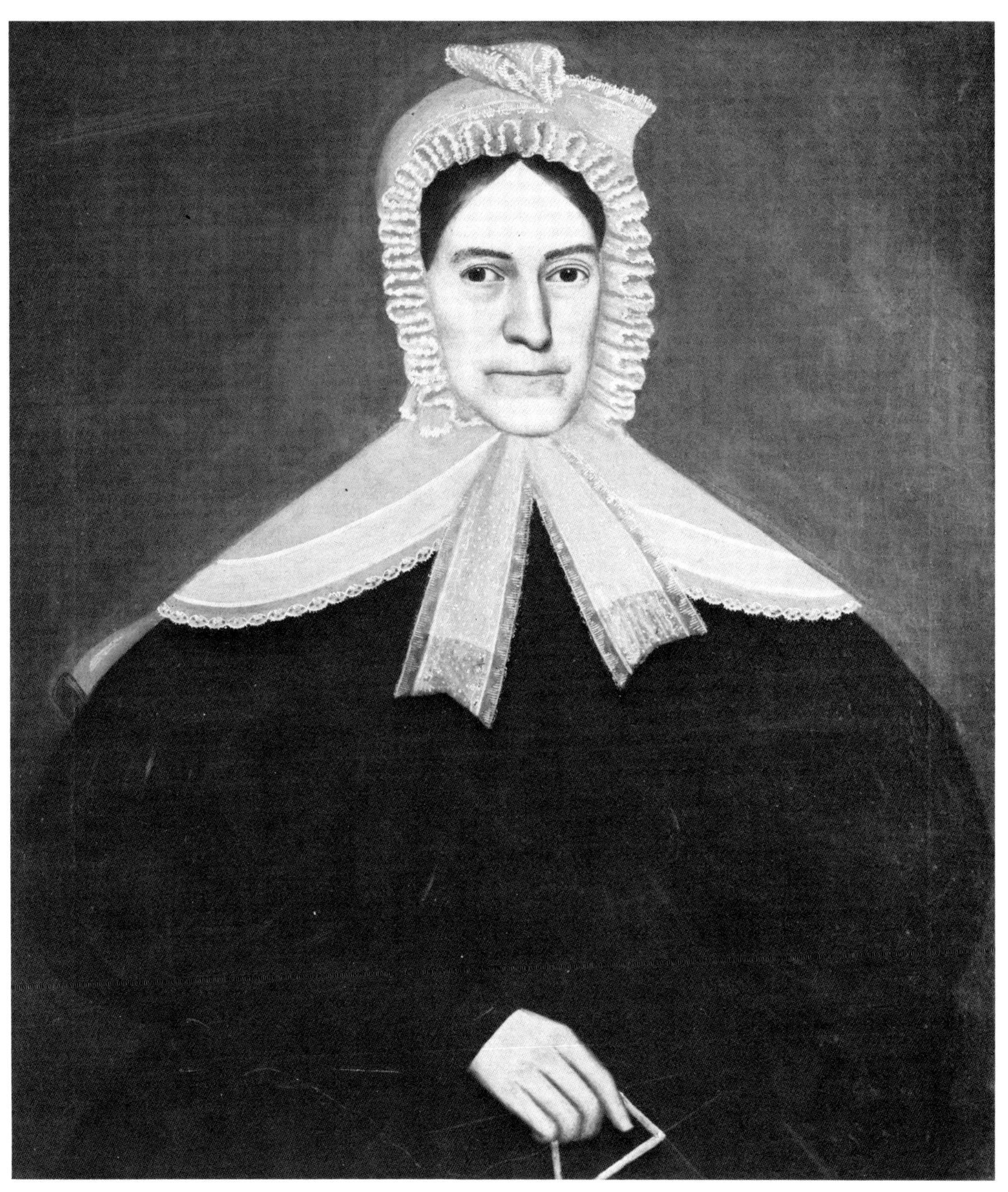

Edward Hicks, American (1780-1849)

The Peaceable Kingdom
Oil on canvas (17-1/2 x 23-3/4 in.) Museum purchase, 1934.65

Hicks was a Quaker minister who made a modest living by sign painting in Bucks County, Pennsylvania. He thought his profession unseemly for a Friend, however, and worried for the state of his soul while engaged in such vain activity. The subject of *The Peaceable Kingdom,* drawn from Isaiah 11:6-9, was his favorite theme both for easel paintings and for utilitarian objects, and he used it also in his sermons. He is thought to have repeated the subject more than a hundred times, always treating it with naive sincerity. In the background here he includes the scene of William Penn negotiating with the Indians, an allusion to a different sort of peaceable kingdom on earth.

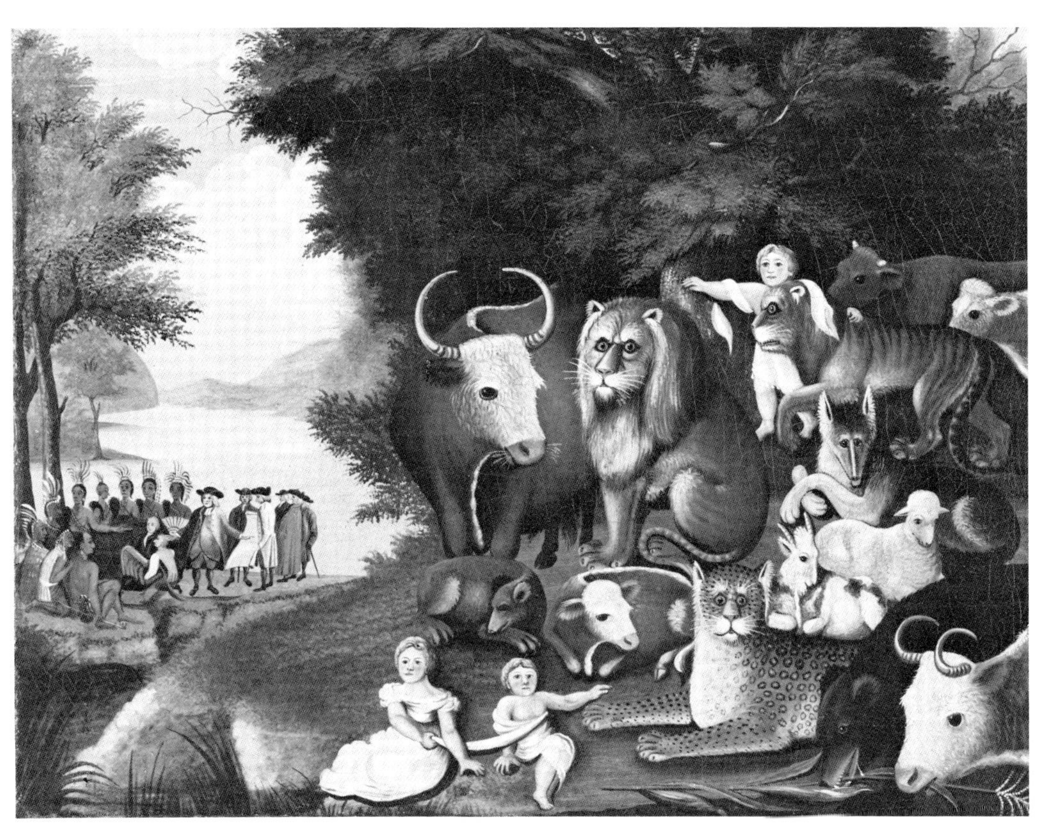

Henry Inman, American (1801-1846)

George Buckham
Oil on canvas, 1839 (34 x 27-1/8 in.) Bequest of Georgianna Buckham Wright, 1921.84

The art of Henry Inman forms a link between the frontier era and the mid-century. A pupil of John Wesley Jarvis (1781-1840), Inman was for a time considered to be the best of American portraitists. He was born in Utica, New York, but moved to New York City in 1812 to become Jarvis' assistant. Inman remained in New York for the rest of his life except for a brief trip to England in 1844 and a three-year stay in Philadelphia in the 1830s. By 1823 Inman was an independent portrait painter of some success. His style still showed traces of Stuart's influence, but was infused with a strong dose of the new realistic attitude, anticipating the rise of photography.

This portrait of George Buckham and a companion picture of his wife Anna Traphagen Buckham and their daughter Georgianna were both painted in New York in 1839. The paintings hung together in the Buckham home for many years until 1919, when the pair was divided between the Worcester Art Museum and the Museum of Fine Arts, Boston. Inman's crisp and somewhat hard style seems well suited to the image of the prosperous, proud, and serious George Buckham.

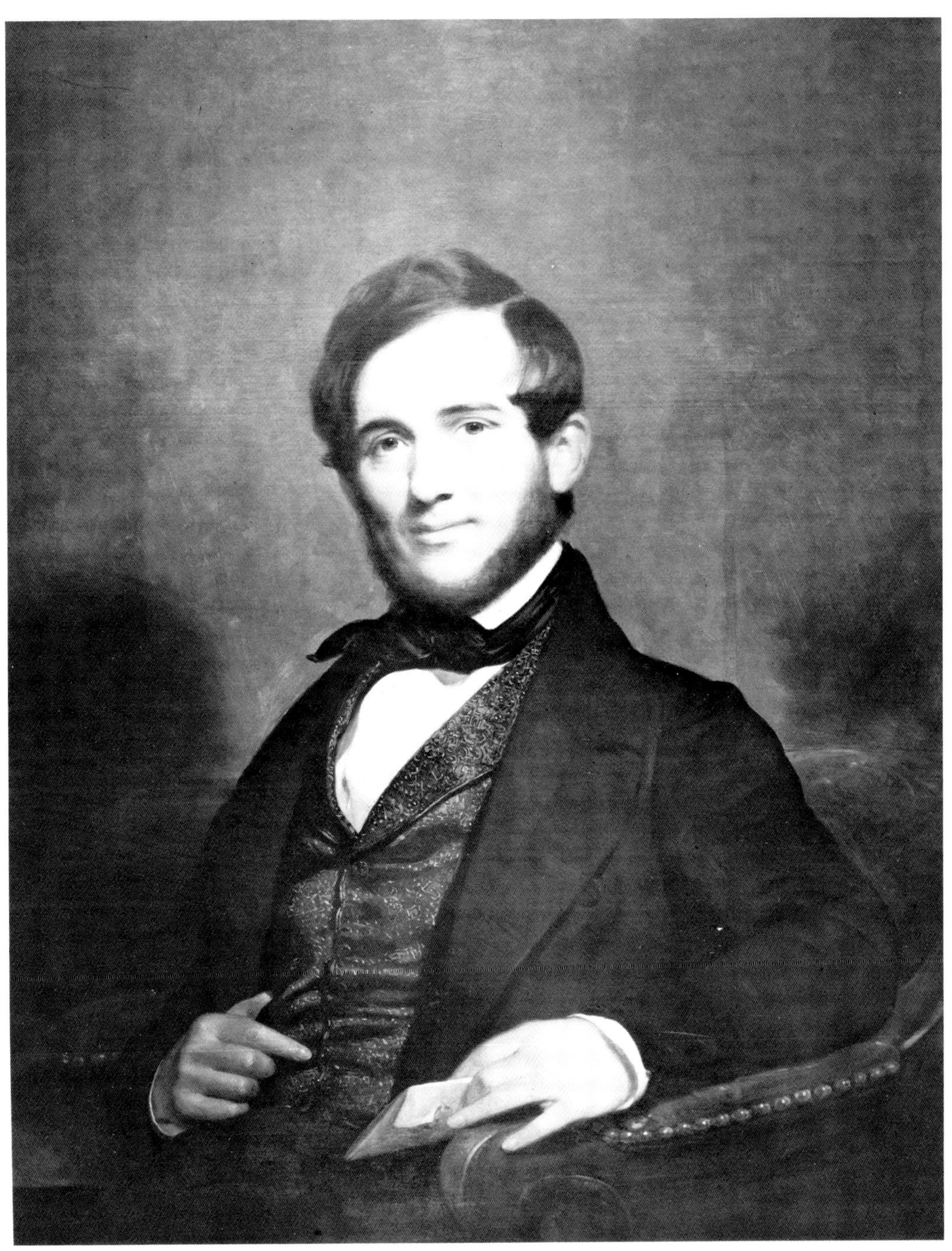

Asher Brown Durand, American (1796-1886)

The Capture of Major André
Oil on canvas, 1833 (25-1/8 x 30-1/2 in.) Museum purchase, 1933.161

Durand was a largely self-taught artist who began his career as an engraver. He took up painting as a pastime, at first concentrating on portraiture. After 1836 he gave up engraving, and later became a leader of the American landscape school. This painting marks a turning point in his career, being probably his first attempt at history painting and at combining figures with landscape. It was painted in 1833.

The event commemorated is the capture of the British officer John André by American militiamen after he had conspired with Benedict Arnold at West Point in 1780. It was the subject of considerable discussion and romanticization in America after the Revolution, and it was a popular subject in art. This composition quickly became the standard one for the theme and was frequently copied. A line engraving after this painting was published by the American Art Union in 1846, and contributed to the dissemination of the image.

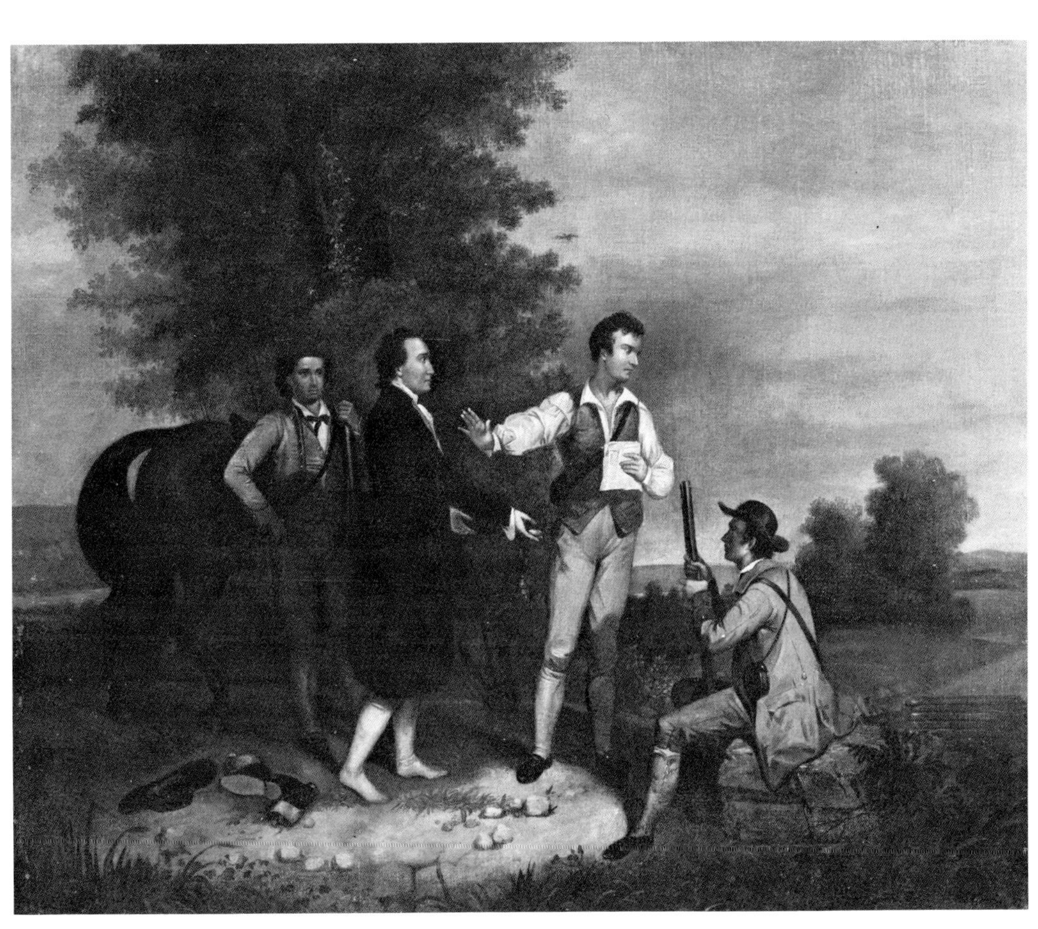

Thomas Cole, American, b. England (1801-1848; lived in America after 1819)

Angels Ministering to Christ in the Wilderness
Oil on canvas, 1843 (72-3/8 x 57-3/8 in.) Museum purchase, 1970.118

Thomas Cole was the major figure in the history of nineteenth-century American painting, a leader in the development of landscape painting, and one of the founders of the Hudson River School. By 1843, when this canvas was painted, he had achieved national recognition for his landscapes and allegorical cycles. He recorded his dissatisfaction with what he had produced, however, and his desire to paint something more significant, a major painting on a scriptural subject.

The painting as originally completed was considerably larger and included on the left a view of the devil, slinking away after his encounter with Christ. Thus, the whole painting illustrated Matthew 4:11: "Then the devil leaveth him, and, behold, angels came and ministered unto him." Cole exhibited the work in that form but was not satisfied and later divided it into two parts. This one, the larger, hung in his home in Catskill, New York, until fairly recently. The left-hand section, entitled *The Tempter,* is owned by the Baltimore Museum of Art.

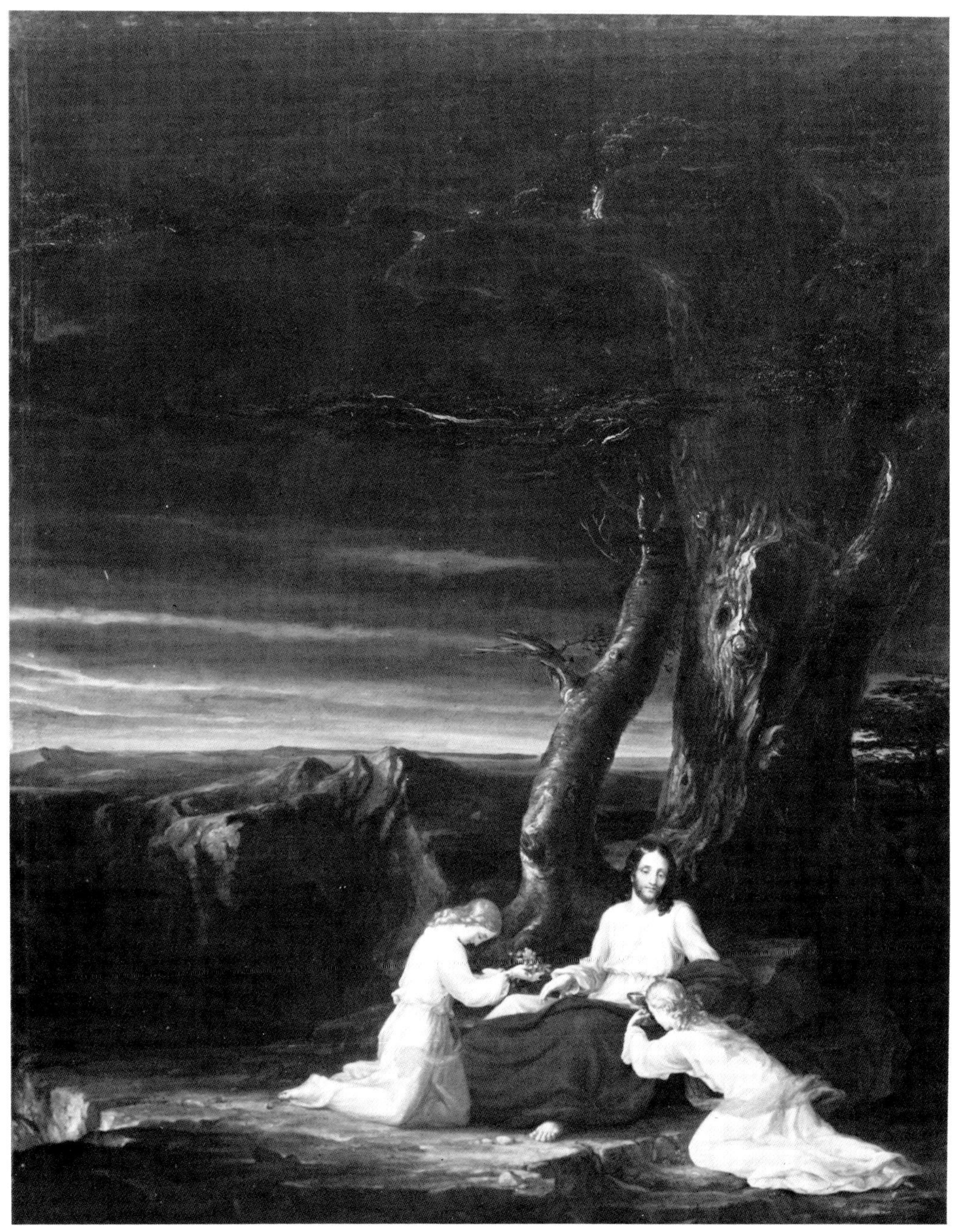

George Loring Brown, American (1814-1889; lived in Europe c. 1839-1859)

View of an Aqueduct in the Campagna near Rome
Oil on canvas, 1842-1843 (32-1/4 x 40-1/2 in.) Gift of Miss Rosamond Thaxter, 1976.186

Brown was a Massachusetts artist who spent several years in Rome. He had connections in Worcester and painted this picture on a commission from Isaac Davis, who was twice mayor of this city. An inscription on the reverse dates the painting 1842-1843.

This painting, in showing a panoramic landscape with ancient ruins, peopled with simple peasants and lit by a golden, setting sun, repeats a familiar Italianate formula. It is a type of painting which was extremely popular with wealthy tourists, and many artists in Italy, both natives and visitors like Brown, specialized in such views. Brown's treatment of the theme has a vitality which may be thought peculiarly American.

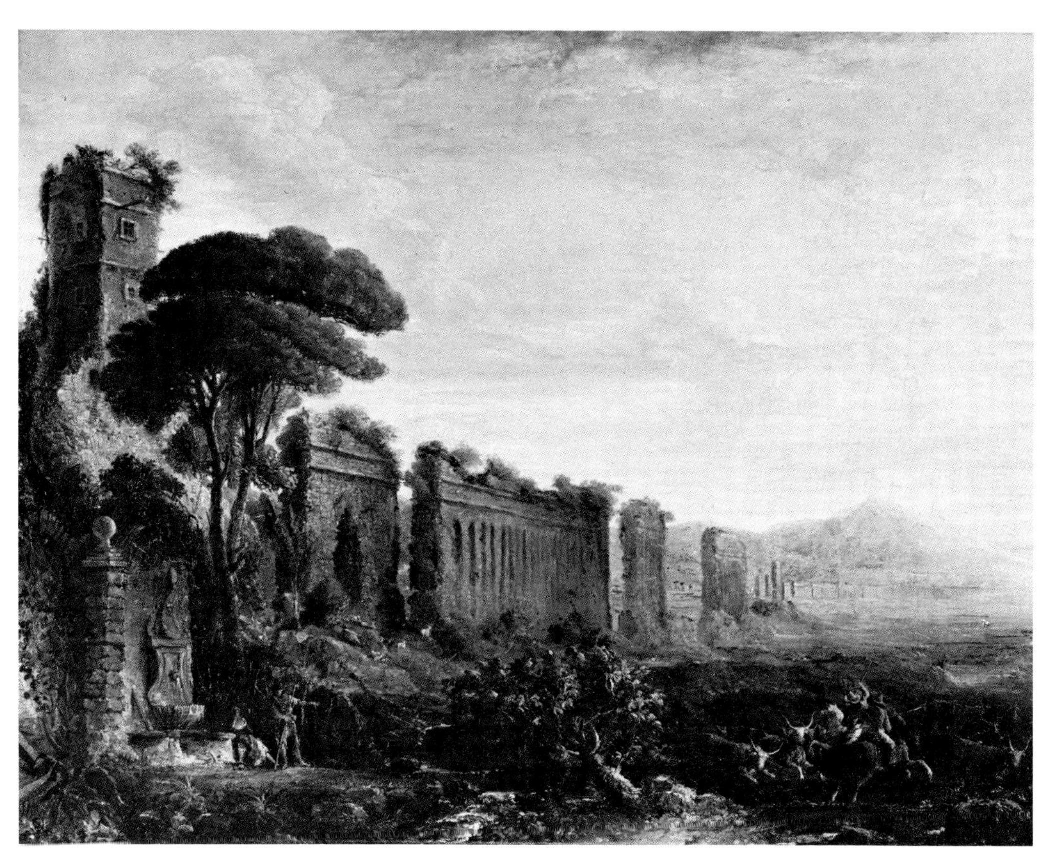

Worthington Whittredge, American (1820-1910)

View of Cincinnati
Oil on canvas, c. 1845 (28-3/8 x 40-1/4 in.) Museum purchase, 1943.3

Worthington Whittredge studied painting in Düsseldorf and Rome, then returned to the United States to join the Hudson River School of landscape painters. This painting, however, was executed prior to his European studies, at a time when he was entirely self-taught and his experience was limited to house and sign painting. He had grown up in a frontier region in Ohio, and was determined to become a landscape painter to record the grandeur and the simpler beauties of his country. This painting reflects that early ambition and shows a remarkably sophisticated handling of light, color, and perspective by an untrained artist.

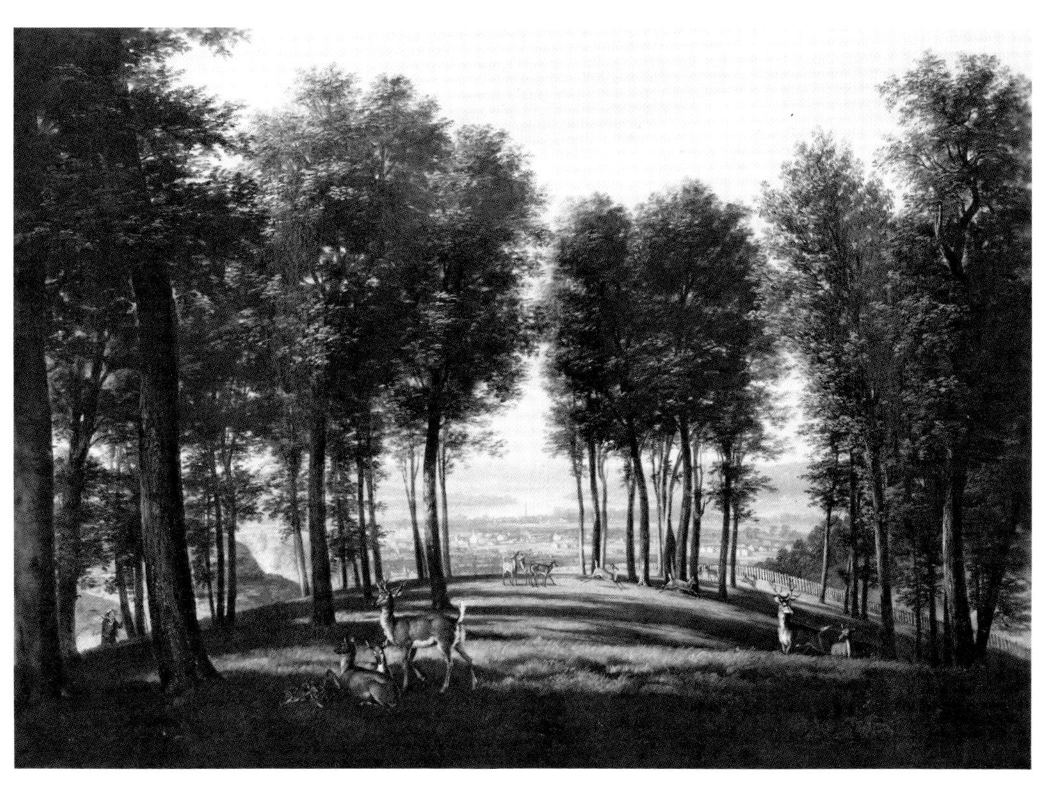

John Frederick Kensett, American (1816-1872)

Conway Valley, New Hampshire
Oil on canvas, 1854 (32-3/4 x 48 in.) Museum purchase, 1961.34

Kensett was a New Englander who received his formal training in Europe between 1839 and 1847 and then returned to America to become one of the foremost members of the Hudson River School of landscapists. He had a successful career from his studio in New York, specializing in panoramic landscapes based on sketches he had drawn from nature.

The exact location of this vista has not been identified, but its traditional title, *Conway Valley, New Hampshire,* may be correct. Kensett is known to have spent summers in that area. The painting, which is considered to be one of the artist's strongest, exhibits the grand romantic conception and powerful luminosity characteristic of the Hudson River School.

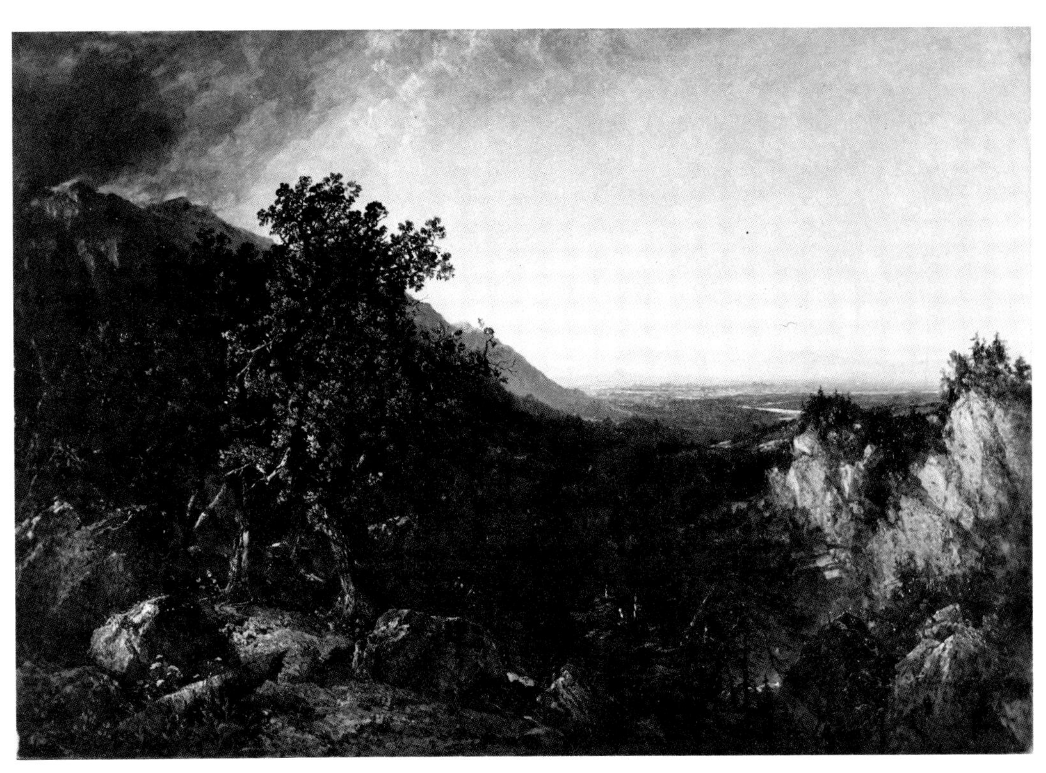

George Peter Alexander Healy, American (1813-1894; lived in Europe 1867-1892)

Henry Wadsworth Longfellow and his Daughter, Edith
Oil on canvas, 1869 (57-1/2 x 42-7/8 in.) Gift of Mrs. J. F. Bowers, 1972.141

George Peter Alexander Healy was one of the few Americans to study in France in the early years of the century. In fact, his period of formal study, in the studio of the painter Gros, was a short one, but his portraits attracted the attention of King Louis-Philippe, and thus began his highly successful career as a portraitist on both sides of the Atlantic. Healy's portrait of the poet Longfellow and his daughter was painted in Rome, where the painter lived from 1867 to 1892.

The portrait is typical of Healy's late work in its rather somber monumentality. Everything about it, from the brushwork to the figures themselves, seems massive and heavy; there is none of the liveliness that could be found in Chester Harding's portraits. But there is also a richness in the handling of light and shade, particularly in the girl's dress and in the contrast of her golden hair with the white mane of the poet. The combination of broad but restrained brushwork and luminous highlights in a generally dark color scheme also appears in the work of the French painter Couture, Healy's fellow-student in Gros' studio and his lifelong friend; possibly Couture influenced Healy in this late work, as he influenced numerous younger American painters.

This portrait study was a gift to the Worcester Art Museum from a great-granddaughter and namesake of the Edith in the painting. It had previously been exhibited at the Longfellow House in Cambridge, Massachusetts.

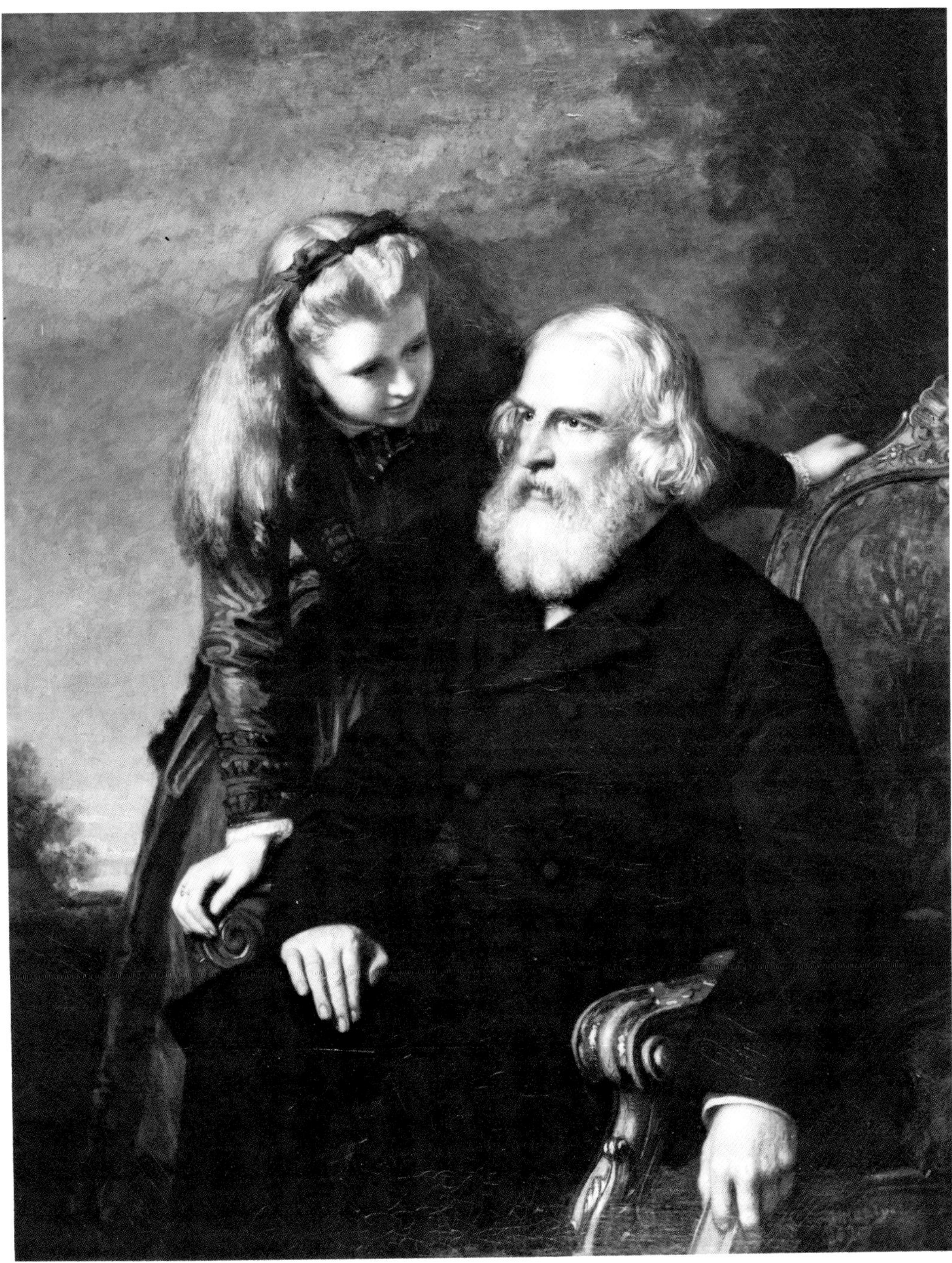

Thomas Eakins, American (1844-1916)

Study of the Head of Dr. S. D. Gross
Oil on canvas, c. 1875 (24-1/8 x 18-1/4 in.) Museum purchase, 1929.124

Eakins was a native of Philadelphia, where he lived and worked most
of his life, after a brief period in the studio of Jean-Léon Gérôme in
Paris. His continuing interest was in portraying human activities with
realism and scientific precision, and he was known especially for his
accurate and almost brutally honest portraits. In spite of this concern
for real appearance, however, his works retain a deep sense of em-
pathy with his sitters.

This sketch is a study for one of Eakins' most famous and successful
works, the *Gross Clinic.* Painted in 1875, it shows Dr. Samuel David
Gross of the Jefferson Medical College in the midst of a lecture-
demonstration in a surgical amphitheater. The sketch, painted quickly
with a palette knife, seems to capture the assurance and knowledge as
well as the features of the famous surgeon.

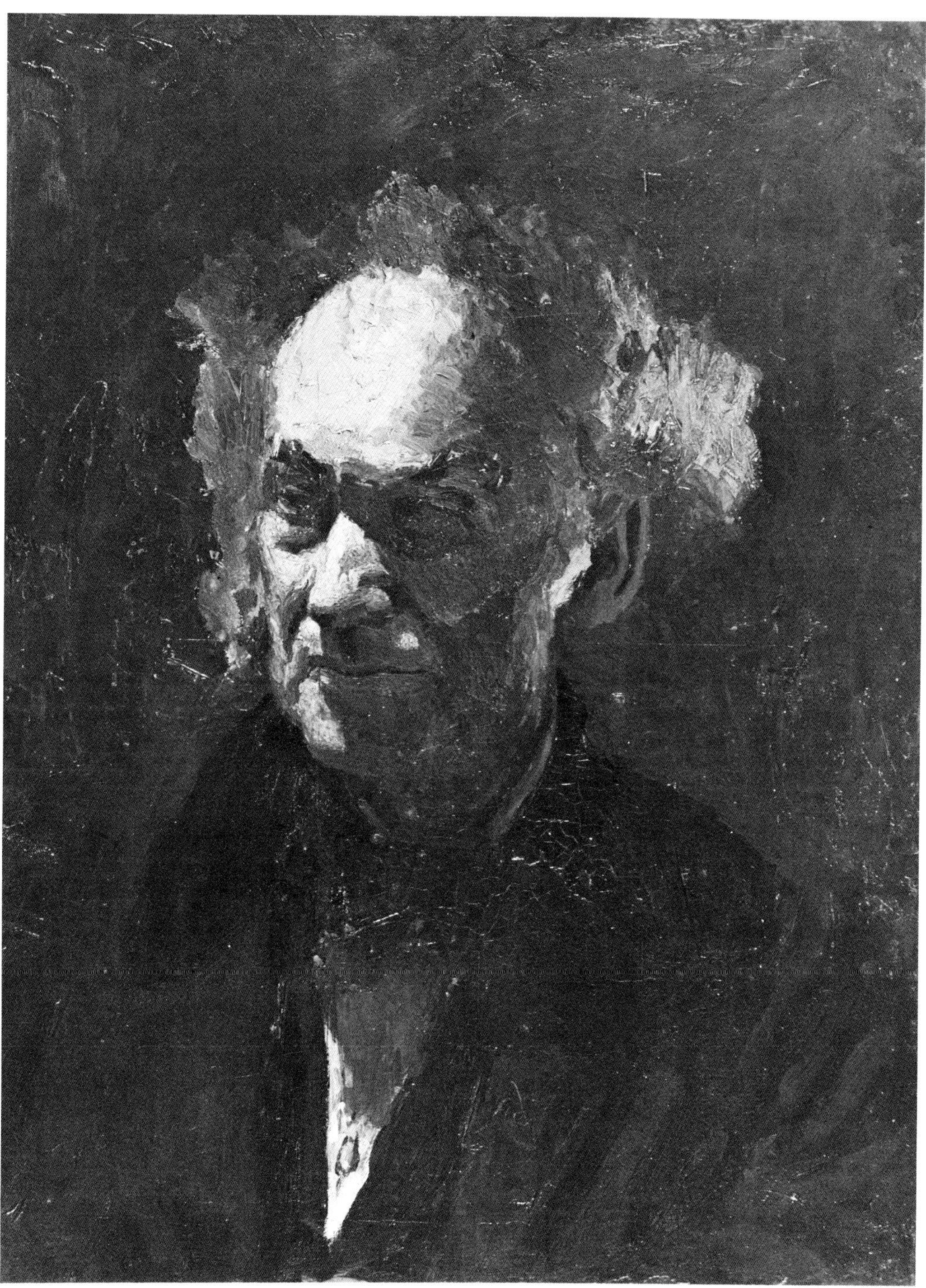

James Abbott McNeill Whistler, American (1834-1903; lived in Europe after 1855)

Arrangement in Black and Brown: The Fur Jacket
Oil on canvas, 1877 (76-3/8 x 36-1/2 in.) Museum purchase, 1910.5

Born in Lowell, Massachusetts, Whistler went to Paris in 1855 to study art, and for the rest of his life was a resident of England and France. He was initially influenced by the French realist painter, Courbet, whose friend he became, and his early development parallels that of the Impressionists. But in 1859 he settled in London, and his later career developed more or less independently of French painting. While the Impressionists were attempting to render the effects of brilliant sunshine, Whistler was painting scenes of fog and twilight in which he could indulge his preference for pale, delicate harmonies of color.

The title of this painting is a typical one for Whistler. It expresses his conviction that a painting should be first and foremost a decorative arrangement of shapes and colors on a flat surface, and only secondarily a representation of reality. This idea, which Whistler probably derived in part from his delight in the decorative patterns of Japanese prints, was to become increasingly influential in the later nineteenth century, and in the years after 1900 would lead to the first completely abstract paintings. Whistler himself always retained a recognizable subject in his pictures; *Arrangement in Black and Brown* is in fact a portrait of his mistress Maud Franklin. But the identity of the figure is less important than the elegance with which its slim shape is placed within the tall, narrow rectangle of the frame, or the way in which the whole shape of the jacket is suggested by the single line of its fur border.

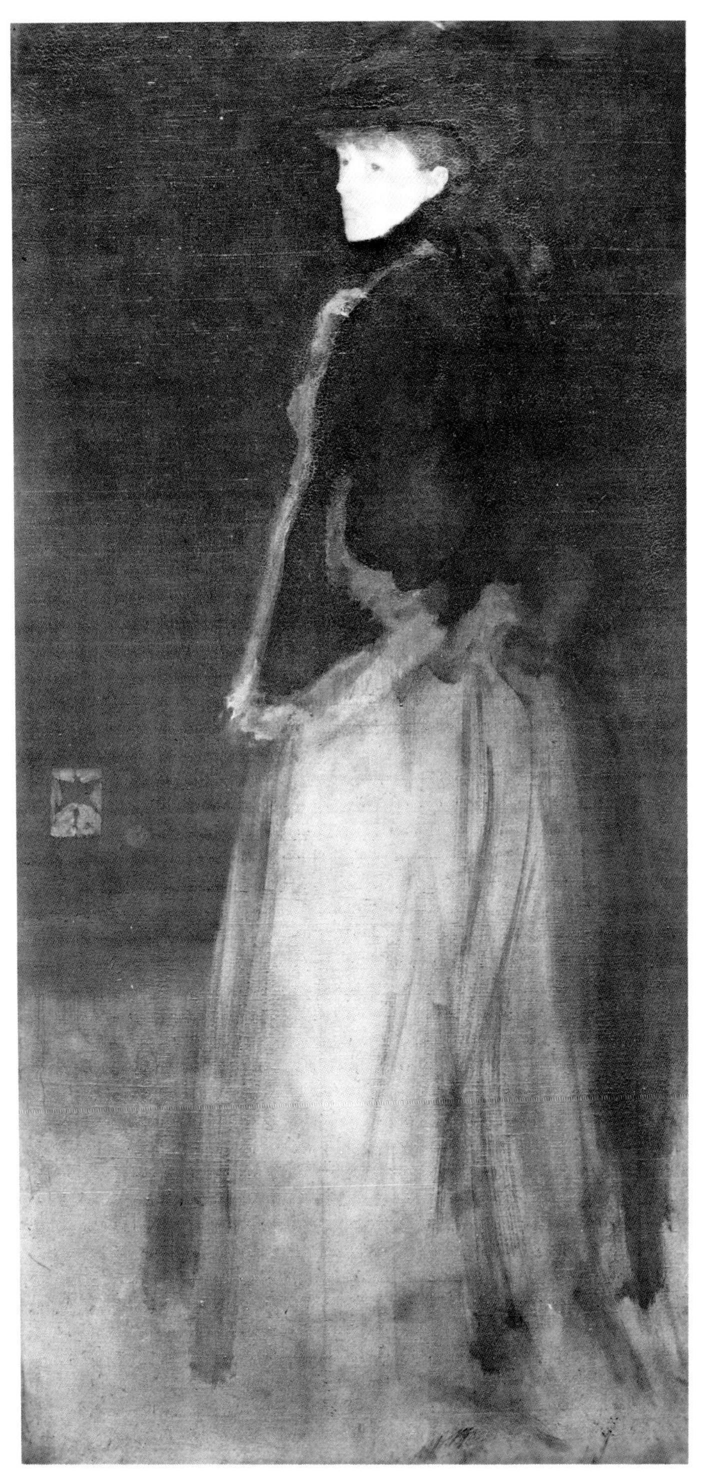

Childe Hassam, American (1859-1935)

Columbus Avenue, Rainy Day
Oil on canvas, 1885 (17-1/8 x 21-1/8 in.) Bequest of Charlotte E. W. Buffington, 1935.36

After a short career in commercial art and illustration, Hassam studied painting in Boston. He made a trip to Europe in 1883, painting in England, Holland, Spain, and Italy, but his painting was more strongly influenced by the years he spent studying and painting in France, from 1886 to 1889. In France he came to know the work of the Impressionists, and he is probably the most talented of the American painters who adopted the Impressionist style of painting.

This painting of Columbus Avenue in Boston dates from just before Hassam's trip to France and shows no direct influence of French painting. The mellow brown tone of the picture, the choice of a misty, wet day, and the delicate blurring of the far distance, all show the influence of Whistler, whose work Hassam could have seen in England and whose modified Impressionism was accepted in England and America sooner than the Impressionism of Monet or Pissarro.

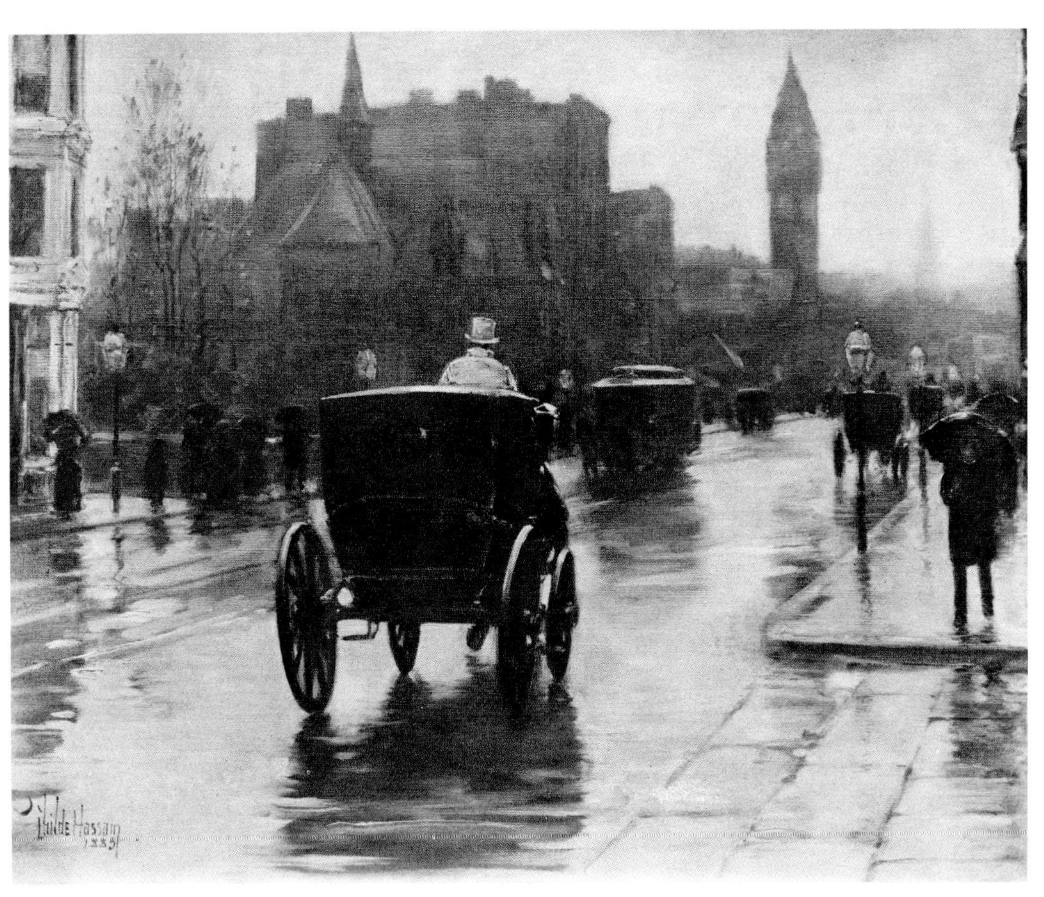

Mary Cassatt, American (1844-1926; lived in France after 1872)

Reine Lefebvre holding a Nude Baby
Oil on canvas, c. 1902 (26-7/8 x 22-5/8 in.) Museum purchase, 1909.15

Mary Cassatt was born in Pittsburgh, heiress to a railroad fortune, but she went to Europe in 1868 to study art and there spent the rest of her life. After a few years in Italy she moved to Paris, where she gained a place in the circle of Degas and was recognized as a leading figure in post-Impressionism.

This painting, which was formerly entitled *Mother and Child,* was probably painted in 1902. The model, Reine Lefebvre, appears in many of Cassatt's paintings of that year. She was a village girl of about sixteen, and the child she holds here is not her own. Still, the artist has captured a warmth and intimacy between them, as well as a shimmering richness of color and texture.

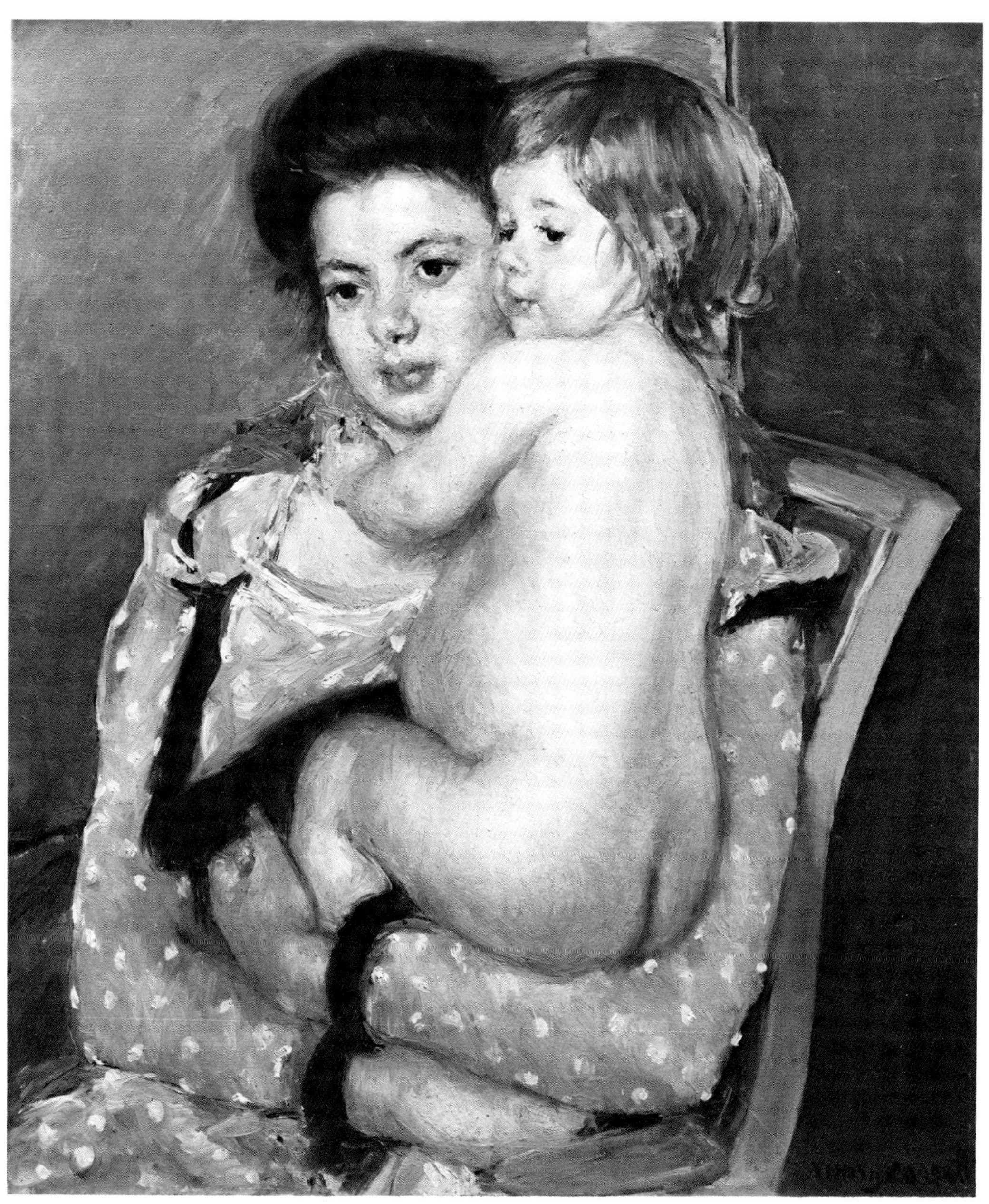

INDEX